YOUNG MONEY:

A Powerful 5 Step Money Plan
to Financial Success Now

YOUNG MONEY:
A POWERFUL 5 STEP MONEY PLAN TO FINANCIAL SUCCESS NOW

by Todd Romer

ISBN 978-0-9883471-6-8

www.networlding.com

YOUNG MONEY

A Powerful 5 Step Money Plan to Financial Success Now

TODD ROMER

TABLE OF CONTENTS

This book is designed to provide accurate and authoritative information on the subject of personal finance and financial success. While all the stories and anecdotes described in the book are based on true experiences, some of the names are pseudonyms, and some situations have been changed slightly for educational purposes and to protect the individual's privacy. This book is sold with the understanding that neither the Author or Publisher is engaged in rendering legal, accounting or other professional services by publishing this book. As each individual financial situation is unique, questions relevant to personal finance and specific to the individual should be addressed to an appropriate professional to ensure that the situation has been evaluated carefully and appropriately. The Author and Publisher specifically disclaim any liability, loss, or risk which is incurred as a consequence, directly or indirectly of the use and application of any of the contents of this book and work.

DEDICATION

This book is dedicated to my wife, Jacquelyn, who has supported my dream for over 15 years while believing in and praying for me along the way. While there have been many hills and valleys on this journey I am grateful to walk through them with you. To my three sons, Jack, Luke and Alec, and my daughter Mia...thank you for your ongoing and unconditional love and encouragement. It has been fun to share my lessons and experiences of life and business along the way to help you navigate your future. Keep in mind the only failure in life is simply not trying. I learn from each of you often and excited about how you will impact the lives of others going forward.

ACKNOWLEDGEMENTS

I decided to launch my first business (Young Money magazine) in 1999, and to still be standing during a wild and crazy ride is incredible and yet humbling at the same time. I have been helped and supported by so many people. Without them none of this ride would still be happening.

Ultimately, this book is dedicated to my wife Jacquelyn and to my four kids, Jack, Luke, Alec and Mia. I am blessed to have each of you in my life. Never stop dreaming and being of service to others.

To my Mom. If you Google the word "generosity" your photo will be there. Thank you for everything you have taught me when it comes to being generous with resources and time that God gives all of us. Thank you for providing an atmosphere of love, encouragement and support growing up. Not once did you ever tell me "I can't do something". You reinforced that I had what it takes to accomplish any goal and I have passed this on to my kids. You and Dad taught me the value of a solid work ethic, to be honest with people, to stick together as a family and so much more.

To my Dad. While he is no longer with us he instilled in me a "never give up attitude" that I lean on to this day. He provided for me and my six siblings generously and he taught me to not take life too seriously nor concern myself with impressing other people. And of course, thanks for showing me how to buy my first stock, Johnson & Johnson at age 15 which was the impetus toward developing a passion to help young people achieve financial success over time.

To my brothers, Bill, Doug, Greg, Mark and my two sisters Jenny and Maria and to my "outlaws". When I decided to leave my nice cushy corporate job many years ago not one of you said I was "crazy". Well, at least not to my face! Your ongoing support and encouragement continue to fuel me.

So many people have been instrumental over the years in supporting and encouraging me to fight the good entrepreneurial fight and to stick to my passion of helping people change their money beliefs and attitudes. Thank you to Al Duarte, Daniel Jimenez, Javier Rodriquez, Becky Stiehl, Bob Barrett, John Fees, Ed Johnson, Alyssa Becker, Melissa Wilson, Marty Grunder, John ("Baboo") Schuermann, John Brogan, Greg Laneve, Ken ("Cruiser") Fedor, Kevin Madigan, Jeff Jones and Ila Cordero.

And finally, thank you to the real stars of this journey...you the reader. You have taken it upon yourself to make a decision to change how you think about money, how you manage money and to make a better life for yourself while affecting others along the way. This is the real recipe for living a rich, full and purposeful life.

OVERVIEW

What is Going On?

Chances are you're one of the millions of millennials that aren't getting one of the most important tools you'll need to succeed in life — money management.

There is little knowledge, capability and confidence when it comes to money management and the pursuit of long term financial success. If you're not worried about money, or think you've got a handle on what to do with it, consider this research:

- 1,000 first-year college students scored an average of 65 percent or a D on a traditional grading scale on the Inceptia National Financial Aptitude Analysis in 2012.
- 85% percent of college grads plan to move back home after graduating.[1] The rate has risen from 67 percent in 2006.[2]
- 93% percent of American parents with teenagers report worrying that their children might make financial missteps, such as overspending or living beyond their means.[3]
- 86% of college students would rather learn about money before making real world mistakes.[4]

How did this happen? Over the last 15 years, corporations, nonprofits, and government entities have spent well over a billion dollars teaching financial literacy. But they're seeing little, if any, change in financial knowledge, capability and aptitude. Our research has discovered the following problems:

- The training has not been the right training—it's not being supported with specific financial behavioral change action steps.
- I mean no disrespect to those conducting training now, but the training is *boring*!
- The training hasn't focused on what matters— the core component of an effective program. I'll share this important aspect in the next chapter.
- Young millennials want to be financially success not necessarily financially literate. So they want to know exactly what to do when it comes to saving, managing, spending and investing money differently.

But there is good news! Young adults do have the desire to become more financially healthy and to learn how to create wealth over time. In fact, according to YPulse Lifeline (2013), 97% of Millennials want to plan more for their future. Research has shown that as student loan debt increases to all-time highs, Millennials will have more interest in personal finance.[5] Even better, how to save for retirement, basic investing, and how loans work were the top three topics Millennials wish they had learned more about in school.[6]

A recent survey of 65,000 college students shows the need and interest to have financial education administered early on in the college experience to maximize the likelihood that students will make sound financial decisions and increase their chance of degree completion.[7]

My Own Story: How I Became Interested In Financial Success

Before we begin, I'd like to tell you more about myself and how I became interested in managing my finances and investing. Like many of you, I didn't receive much formal education about saving, investing, and planning for my financial future. But with the support of my father, mother, and some difficult and expensive lessons and experiences along the way, I figured it out.

I distinctly remember one Saturday morning in September of 1982 at my family's home in Dayton, Ohio. I was a sophomore in high school and it was a Saturday morning. I sat at the kitchen table eating cereal for breakfast and perusing the sports page of our local newspaper as my Dad was using a magnifying glass to read a section of the paper. Intrigued by whatever had captured his attention so fully, I asked my Dad what he was looking at. He told me he was checking his stocks. I did not understand what stocks were, so I continued eating in silence.

Suddenly, Dad asked, "So how much money did you make cutting grass this past summer?"

"Uh, about $3,000," I responded, not sure where this conversation was going.

"You need to start investing in stocks now," he advised me.

My Dad told me I should buy 10 shares of Johnson & Johnson. I had no idea what he was talking about. I asked him what Johnson & Johnson was and if they were people. He laughed a bit. Of course, he explained that it was a company that manufactures, distributes and sells Tylenol and Johnson's Baby Shampoo, as well as many other products all across the globe. Now, Tylenol and Johnson's Baby Shampoo were products I knew. I had used both and understood what they did and how popular they were.

The very next week, I purchased 10 shares of Johnson & Johnson, or JNJ stock, at $43.00 per share for a total investment of $430 plus a brokerage commission of $75.00. As a point of reference that same stock purchase (trade) today would cost around $7.00 in commission. I certainly felt proud of my newly acquired financial acumen and that I was now an "investor". It felt good and different and I liked it.

Several weeks later, however, the entire nation was in a state of panic. Someone had walked into a pharmacy in Chicago and replaced some Tylenol capsules with capsules laced with cyanide. Seven people died as a result. Tylenol went from being the nation's most popular painkiller to being a source of fear for an entire nation. Many people predicted that Tylenol would never recover.

The stock price of JNJ plummeted nearly 25% in one day and I was angry with my Dad for encouraging me to invest in JNJ. I had worked hard for the $430.00 I'd invested, and I wanted to get out and sell this stock. When I asked him how to rid myself of this bad investment, my Dad laughed and told me it was a good time to buy more stock in JNJ. I thought he was crazy. Sadly, I did not take his advice to purchase more stock in JNJ, but I'm happy to say that I did not sell my shares either.

My investment paid off in much bigger ways than I anticipated. Just a few years later, I was a senior at the University of Dayton. One day, my brokerage statement came in the mail. I was shocked and thrilled to see that my investment of $430.00 had grown to nearly $2,000.00 over the course six years. I learned a powerful lesson that day: that my money was working for me. And the best part of all was I did not have to do anything to earn this money, apart from investing the initial amount. I was so excited. And the truth is, aside from one childhood friend, nobody I knew from high school or college was investing in stocks. It seemed like such easy money that I just could not understand why all my friends weren't investing.

Each year in high school and throughout college, I earned between $4,000 and $7,000 over the summer cutting lawns, painting houses and doing small landscaping jobs. After investing in JNJ, I began to purchase stocks in other well-known companies including shares in Coca Cola, Citizen Utilities, Dayton Power and Light and General Electric. After hearing my older brothers discussing mutual funds, I started reading about mutual funds, eventually investing in the Nicholas Fund, Mutual Series Fund, and the T. Rowe Price Science and Technology Fund.

These investments were paying off over time as I paid cash for two cars in a span of six years. My first car was a Chevrolet Cavalier that I bought for $4,500 from my cousin that was in excellent shape, had low miles, power locks, power windows, and an Alpine stereo. These features were a big deal back in 1988. My second car was an Acura Legend that I paid $9,000 in cash two years out of college. The money for both of these cars came from my investments of five or more years in stocks and mutual funds. Investing was exciting, and I wanted more.

A couple of years out of college, I eventually found a job in medical sales. I continued to seek more information about money and investing. I was continually surprised that there was not a magazine or a simple book specifically for young people like me about investing. At that time, *Money, Smart Money,*

Worth, and Kiplinger's magazine were important, popular sources of information about personal finance and investing for adults. I bought these magazines to learn of their stock tips and advice about investing in stocks. However, the other personal finance content these magazines offered was way over my head and of no relevance for me. It was frustrating.

Young Money Magazine Launches From My Basement

I realized that young people needed more information about investments and money management in general. They needed a publication just for them. So in 1999, I left my job in medical sales to launch *Young Money* Magazine. After creating this magazine from the basement of my home in Cincinnati, *Young Money* was immediately successful, receiving substantial media coverage, including on the front page of the Money section of *USA Today*, along with coverage in the *Washington Post, Cincinnati Enquirer, Sacramento Bee, Inc. Magazine,* and many other big city newspapers. Between 1999 and 2009, nearly seven million copies of *Young Money* were published and distributed on 200+ college campuses.

I lived what I thought was an amazing life in my mid-20s. I was newly married to an amazing woman. We had two healthy, happy sons, a newly built home with a 25% down payment on the mortgage, and my Acura was paid for. Life was good, but I never had a real sense of joy or peace. I was always wanting. Wanting to earn and have more, and this attitude began to rob me of contentment. My mental and unwritten goal became to simply acquire enough money so that I could "retire" at a young age. I believed the popular lie that my wealth would one day bring me true happiness.

About the time that *Young Money* Magazine was launched, the Internet began to boom. Internet startup companies were popping up by the dozens and Americans saw them as the hottest investments. Stocks like Amazon, Yahoo, and Broadcast. com were nearly doubling and sometimes tripling in value every six months or less. My heart was still in *Young Money,* but the overnight millionaires made by internet ventures and those who owned their stock were grabbing my attention.

I proceeded to take the money I had invested in solid, well-known companies and mutual funds and invest it in companies that had only been around a couple of years and were only recently publicly traded stocks. To my dismay, I ended up losing nearly 40% of my net worth in what turned out to be fly-by-night stocks. At the time, I was devastated and embarrassed, but the entire crash, loss, and disappointment turned out to be one of the greatest blessings in disguise. This situation forced me to acknowledge that money had wormed its way to become the number one priority in my life. It was a wakeup call. I realized that money on its own was not enough to make me or anyone else happy. I reoriented and prioritized, as my driving mission became assisting young people with making responsible financial decisions, which could not only affect their lives down the road in dramatic fashion, but the lives of others as well.

Young Money Magazine was relatively successful, but like many startup companies, it still had its cash flow issues. After publishing the magazine for several years under two different ownership groups, I realized that a traditional magazine was not enough to create the kind of change I was looking for. I wanted to help young people make better financial choices, based on specific behavioral actions steps that would lead to financial health. As the Internet grew and the digital landscape changed, particularly in reaching a young adult market, it made more sense to stop publishing the magazine and shift my focus. And so in 2010, the Young Money LIVE! campus event and speaking tour was born. Since then, Young Money LIVE! has visited over 300 college and university campuses across the nation. We're now focused on providing a relevant financial success pathway for any millennial to follow so they can begin to live a life that fits their dreams. The 5 Step Plan to Financial Success.

What You Can Expect From This Book

This book goes against the grain of traditional personal finance education to some extent. Let me explain. In Chapter 5, I focus on the importance of giving as part your personal financial plan. What does giving have to do with becoming financially successful you may ask? Actually, it has quite a bit to do with it. This book not only gives you specific direction on how to change financial behavioral and to create wealth over time, but also teaches and hopefully inspires you to live a much richer life by positively affecting others along the way. Are you ready? Let's get started.

CHAPTER 1: STEP ONE
Make a Decision to Dream

Making a decision to dream may sound like a fluffy or strange first step to achieving financial health and wealth, but it's absolutely essential to the plan I will share with you throughout this book. In fact, it's the foundation to becoming financially successful. What I find is that most people are just wandering through life and afraid to dream real dreams because of good old fashioned fear. Fear paralyzes all of us from time to time. But when you truly make a conscious decision to dream like never before you will slowly conquer many facets of fear and your life takes on a whole different meaning. *→vision board*

Financial health is critical to every aspect of your life and your future. Like physical health, your financial health will determine what you can actually do in life. So what is 'financial health' anyway? The next time you're at the beach, or a public swimming pool, look around. What do you see? Buff, hard bodies? Skinny, undeveloped bodies? Maybe there are some people who are a little or a lot overweight. Others are so thin it hurts to look at them. Then there are the handful of folks who look like models. They're fit, muscular, and in shape. They're obviously healthy. They take care of themselves. They are in control of their bodies, their health, and their energy. They're aware of the importance of diet, exercise, sleep, and work. They know what to eat, when to eat, when to exercise, how much sleep they need, and what their physical limits are. They know what they can and can't do. They're able to fight off illnesses that might bring others down. They're able to work longer and harder because they have a reservoir of strength that comes from long term training. Their hearts, lungs, and brain function at 100 percent because they get enough nutrients, oxygen and rest. In other words, they're very healthy.

Financial health is pretty much the same thing. You're either underweight (broke all the time), overweight (saddled with debt and spending more money than you actually have), or you're putting more demands on your bank account and credit cards than they can handle. You struggle. It's painful. It's also obvious to others, just as your physical condition is when you're wearing nothing but a swimsuit.

Just like you can build your body up, slim down, bulk up, and create a healthy, vibrant physical body, you can do the same with your financial health and body. The healthier you are financially, the farther you can go, the more you can do, and the more fun, relaxed, and influential your life will be.

Figuring Out Your Why?

It's all about your WHY. Your purpose or your WHY around some future goals or dreams ignites the fire and desire in your heart to generate that consistent commitment that will stay with you throughout your journey. It won't be easy, but it will be possible for you to achieve your goals if you stick with your plan. You're going to have ups and downs; there's no doubt about that. It will be much easier to manage both extremes when you anticipate them and realize that small efforts, over time, do add up. As a young person, you have time on your side. That time advantage translates into money wellness.

I have spoken to thousands of young millennials over the last several years on college campuses and many are afraid to dream because of the poor economy. Their fear may also be an extension of past financial struggles within their family growing up. They think that because their parents were not financially successful then they probably won't be either. So, for the most part, they just settle and go through the motions of life. Ugh!

Others are afraid to dream because of the fear of failure. Our culture has not figured out that failure is a good thing. Failure of anything gives us resolve. Failure gives us valuable insight into what we can do differently the next time. Failure breeds introspection and refection. Failure shows us we are actually on the road to getting something right. Finally, failure shows we are a participant in life and not just a spectator. There's not one successful entrepreneur, President or CEO in the world that did not experience failure of some sort. So why would you be afraid to dream because of possible failure? It makes no sense. I have a one word command for you from the bottom of my heart: Dream!

Don't become deterred because you think odds are against you, continue pressing forward. The idea of dreaming and asking "Why" you want to do something—become a doctor, lawyer, teacher, accountant, pastor, entrepreneur, etc., has been the topic of best-selling books, such as Simon Sinek's "Start with

Why." Here, we learn that your "Why" is the catalyst for your life's work and that discovering it, embedding it into your daily life and keeping it as your compass for all of your major life choices, creates a much richer life. I mean richer in the sense of true fulfillment, purpose and personal success—the creation of a more meaningful life. Your number one goal and dream should be to have your "Why" result in making a difference for others. This is because *when* what you are most passionate about makes a difference for others, you will experience a deeper sense of satisfaction. As Adam Grant, a Wharton School of Business professor, shares in his book, *Give and Take*, studies reveal that what drives success in goal achievement for individuals is the direct result of positive feedback from even one personal connection of those whom you are focused on helping.

For example, imagine you are raising money for a fundraising campaign for a local hospital system that is seeking to build a new children's hospital in the area. You're excited to see funds raised as your brother was benefited by a hospital. He was helped by a team of doctors whose great care and attention resulted in a successful life-saving operation. You vowed that when you were able to make a difference for a local hospital, you would do so.

So here you are. You have been dialing for dollars on behalf of the hospital now for three weeks in your spare time. So far your results have been nominal. You aren't at the bottom of the list, but you are nowhere near the top. Although you're attempting to do well, you're not getting the results or satisfaction that you wanted. What's wrong?

You find out that the hospital is holding a session to introduce volunteers to Tommy. Tommy just received a new kidney. You see a video of Tommy's life showing a wide-toothed, grinning, chubby two-year old running without fear throughout his house. His frustrated, but laughing, mother chases him hoping to prevent a bad fall. You laugh at Tommy's clever ability to keep his mom on the run as he runs left and right, faster than she can keep up. He loves the excitement and giggles with glee as she almost catches him, but then misses. At the last minute she bends to scoop him up in her arms, yet he wiggles his body so quickly she loses her grasp.

Then the video switches dramatically. You are in a hospital room. You see a child in a stark white-metal framed hospital bed covered by tubes running inside and out of his small, fragile body. You see a man and the woman you saw before running after Tommy. His mother bends over him. His eyes are vacant; his skin is a pale white. You hear a narrator sharing that this is also Tommy's life. Tommy ended up eating a mushroom as the family was out taking a walk. To their horror the mushroom was poisonous—so poisonous, in fact, that it took out both of his kidneys. Now the vibrant little boy you just saw is now in line for a very risky surgery—a kidney transplant.

The video switches again. You see a team of doctors and surgical nurses flying in on a helicopter. One of the doctors is carrying a small container labeled "human organs." You see an operation and hear the narrator sharing a tense, minute-by-minute story of the progress of Tommy's kidney transplant. Even if the surgery is initially successful, there are no assurances that the kidney won't be rejected later.

Finally, the video switches to a segment that makes you sigh with relief. It's two years later in Tommy's life. Not only has Tommy's body accepted his new kidney, but once again Tommy is a healthy, giggling, and on-the-move four year old. You feel joy well up in your chest. You smile. The video ends. The person who has the voice of the narrator in the movie steps forward. You realize it's the surgeon that handled Tommy's operation. He shares how happy he was to have such a great team at his side the day he gave Tommy his new kidney. He says he is also blessed to get to see the wonderful results of the team's life-saving efforts.

Then he turns and with his right hand he waves someone from outside of the room to come in. All of a sudden, a chubby, red-haired four-year old dashes in. It's Tommy! You feel as if you, in some small way, were responsible for this wonderful outcome. You feel different somehow. You feel connected to the results. So what happens next?

Surprisingly, this brief but personal "make-a-difference" experience *is connected* to how you will perform. Why? Because you have experienced a real life example of what your efforts can result in, and the result is powerful and moving. Imagine how many other Tommy's you can help! As you go back to your calling, you *feel* different about your efforts. You share the story of Tommy with those who take your call. You also don't let those calls where others hang up on you or listen apathetically get to you. You know now that every call counts and that sooner or later, you will get someone who really is touched by your story. You *know* this from the inside out now. You've had first-hand experience seeing what the money you contribute to raising can do for a human life. It's an amazing result. You want to see it happening more.

That's the reward of making a difference. You realize that you can make a big difference in the lives of others without overexerting yourself. If you stick to your Why, your passion, the results you want will follow.

Applying Tommy's Story Further

Just as Tommy's story helps you see the way to connect with your unique "Why" to your new Young Money Plan, the following real stories further expand upon the same concepts.

Take Shareen Rosier, a young woman from Florida Atlantic University in Boca Raton, Florida. Shareen used to think that success could only be attained by the haves and not the have nots. She used to also believe that even if she worked hard she would not acquire a lot of money or achieve some of her long term goals.

She was scared about investing. She had heard stories of how people lost money investing in various things like stocks, real estate or new businesses. She genuinely felt that investing was full of risk with little reward.

But she knew she had to do something—to take some risks with her money. She knew of some successful people. Their success was traced back to them taking some kind of risk. However, she didn't know *how* to go about investing wisely. Her mother had told her often that a good education was the most important thing she could pursue and that if you were well educated you could figure out how to be successful with money. Yet that whole conversation seemed vague and unfinished to her.

Shareen went to private schools growing up. Her family and teachers rarely talked about money let alone how to manage it. If they did talk about it, the focus was on topics like what is a car loan or a savings account. She wanted more.

She was scared before our Young Money LIVE! event because she dreamed of becoming a doctor. However, she felt that if she took that path she would be paying back education loans for the rest of her life and not much money would be left for her. She was stuck and suppressing her dream of medical school because she didn't understand how to manage and invest her money. She was overwhelmed.

After Snapshot

The transition Shareen made is similar to that of the other individuals who have experienced our Young Money LIVE! event and 5 step plan to financial success. Shareen had not realized that money could be managed simply. With a few adjustments in her life, she now saves money automatically each month. She doesn't spend as much on new clothes as she did before, but she is happy with the clothes she does have. She came to realize that she didn't miss the new clothes as much because she knew her savings were taking her toward her bigger medical school goal. She additionally mentioned that "fashion changes so quickly anyway!" And she realizes that she will be able to afford fashion in the long run if she sticks to the plan.

Shareen's interest in investing has also grown substantially. She feels her goals are in sight. She also wants to own a business someday—a medical clinic. There she would like to offer affordable healthcare to the community. She also has a heart for kids, a dream that might lead to her owning an adoption agency where she could also offer free medical care while the kids wait to be adopted.

Shareen has also developed a reward system for herself. She rewards herself for accomplishing short-term financial goals, such as saving a certain amount of money for consecutive months.

Before Snapshot

Another story is that of Nav Shergill. Nav was born in India and lived there for 10 years until he moved to Lodi, California. There he attended University of California, Santa Cruz, one of the most beautiful campuses in the U.S. I met him after he attended our event on campus. Nav immediately emailed me afterwards saying he was transformed by the presentation. He shared with me that before attending my presentation, he had a minimum wage job but had no system for managing his money. He did not know money management could be systematic. When he heard about creating an automatic savings, investing, and giving plan he immediately became intrigued. As he put it, he received the HOW information he needed to manage his money.

Before the seminar Nav had no specific financial goals. He always wanted to be financially successful, yet he realized he did not know what that success would look like. His only specific goal was to do well in school. The presentation helped him shift his views about money and immediately drew his interest to begin investing for his future life goals and dreams.

After Snapshot

Now, at 26, Nav wants to start a family and provide them with financial security. Because he started investing and saving at age 23 he has three years of savings already. He continues to build today. His goal is to create personal development programs for young adults and college-aged students in the near future so he can educate youth about what he would have liked to have known when he was younger.

Nav's *Why* is that he "wants to be a good leader of others and his future family." Having financial security is necessary for that to happen. Now he has the confidence to move forward and develop his leadership and personal development program because of the 5 Step Money Plan. Just like Shareen, Nav did not know what he did not know. Now he has a plan.

Before Snapshot

Kelly Rocklein had an interest in nutrition early on and so wanted to be a nutritionist or personal trainer at the time she came to the Young Money LIVE! event. Her thoughts about money were also negative. She thought that greatness or success was for a select few. Her only plan was to go to college, get a degree, and get a "good job." With her goal around nutrition, she also knew she would have to do a lot of studying in science, something that would be difficult for her.

Because her family had limited funds Kelly would have to work during her college years as she had before she started college. As a high school senior, she had worked up to four jobs. She had to do the same early in college.

All she knew about money prior to the workshop was that if she worked hard she would earn enough money to move out on her own. She was confident she could work hard and she wasn't afraid of hard work. She also had a savings account where she saved regularly. That's where her money knowledge stopped. She knew she needed to learn how to grow her money through investing, but she had no clue about how to do it or where to learn it.

After Snapshot

Now Kelly has developed an awareness, understanding, and confidence in investing. She also has a renewed interest in giving which provides her a great feeling. She shared, "My mother always talked about the importance of giving or tithing. I give now not expecting anything in return. What I get in return is a great feeling that I am helping someone somewhere."

She has confidence in pursuing her dream of having enough money to teach yoga classes not for pay, but because she enjoys it. She adds, "With money being invested and working for me my dream of teaching yoga is not to get a paycheck."

Before Snapshot

Jevon Howell was different from Kelly. He didn't really become aware of his need for money accumulation and management until later in college. This was when money started to become more of a focus in his life. It was not as big of a concern for him in high school because he didn't have as many expenses. In college, he found he needed much more money. Unlike Kelly, his goals and dreams were not clear. As he puts it, "I really did not have much drive or motivation."

After Snapshot

Immediately after the seminar at Florida International University, Jevon saw a real way to grow his money and manage it. Before he had not seen or heard of this type of money plan. Knowledge of a money growth process immediately gave him a reason to start dreaming and setting goals. He learned a way to get to those dreams through investing monthly, saving monthly, and monitoring his spending.

He also had a new desire to start investing, and somewhere down the road to start a business. During the seminar, he learned how to make investing less complicated. Jevon added, "The seminar enabled me literally to start dreaming because I saw a money system that I could follow."

Your Financial Success: Set Short Term Goals First

In our culture today, we hear messages like "dream big baby dream big." I obviously want you to dream big given this chapter title but you must set smaller, short term goals and dreams first so you can experience the satisfaction and confidence that goes along with reaching a goal in the first place. If you don't give yourself the opportunity to reach short term goals you may be discouraged from pursuing larger dreams and goals. Many people who have dreamed big only in their minds and did not establish short term goals or "small dreams" first ended up backing down on their big dreams because the road early on got a little rough. Their confidence in themselves took a hit and they made a choice to retreat from their dream.

I launched *Young Money* Magazine with the intent of selling it to Time Inc. I did not set initial short term goals, such as monthly subscriptions or number of advertisers in the magazine after year one. It was discouraging and painful when I didn't reach my only goal, which was only long-term. With short term goals, you'll avoid most discouragement by continually achieving your pursuits one step at a time.

We're all creatures of habit. Our habits are developed through our actions. At first you may not feel happy about sacrificing through saving, even if it's only small amounts of money. But, as you save a little at a time for a short-term goal of say $250 in one month, once you achieve this goal, you will likely have a feeling of satisfaction and some initial but important confidence.

You did it! While your friends were spending money again at Starbucks, Chipotle, the newest burger place or the latest fashion, clothes, music, etc., you were not. Now you have 100 - 200 more dollars than they have. You are ahead of the game when it comes to short term financial health.

Steps 2 and 3 will further explain how can begin to save money differently than what you are probably doing now. Notice the short term goal examples below start with "I will" and not "I want." "I will" statements breed focus and confidence, which is paramount to reaching any goal or dream. And make sure you write down your goals so you can see them often. In addition, make your goals specific and have a deadline. This creates action.

I love what Dave Ramsey says. "Live like no one else now so you can live like no one else later". Such truth.

Examples of Short Term Goals

1. I will set up an automatic savings plan by opening a savings and checking account with a bank or credit union this week.
2. I will save $100 within 30 days and $500 within three months.
3. I will save $2,500 within 6 months for a down payment on a used car.

Examples of Mid Term Goals

Now you can move on to your next set of goals—your mid term goals. These goals lay the foundation for you to continue believing in yourself and getting closer to knowing and pursuing your personal WHY in life. Your mid term goals—1 to 5 years could include the following:

1. I will save $5,000 within 1 year to put toward a new or used car
2. I will save $10,000 - $15,000 in 3 years for a new apartment, furniture and/or trip to Europe
3. I will save $25,000 - $35,000 in 5 years as a down payment on a first home.

This is where you should again start connecting with your "WHY" and apply it to your personal 5 Step Plan to Financial Success. The energy to stay committed will come from recommitting to your purpose or WHY. It's easy to lose sight of your goals. How do you carry your dreams and put them front and center in your life on a daily basis? Life is distracting.

Knowing how to keep your dreams in front of you often is empowering. Following are some ideas for staying committed to your WHY.

- **START JOURNALING.** This small step will go a long way in building a savings habit. Write in your journal daily. In fact, write in it the first thing every morning, even if it's only for one minute. Write down the amount you have saved. For example, "I have already saved $100 and I am working toward now saving $300. I am grateful that I continue to save and I am committed to reaching all of my goals."
- **LOOK IN THE MIRROR DAILY AND STATE YOUR COMMITMENT.** Don't take this step lightly; looking into your own eyes and making a commitment to yourself will have a powerful effect on you. It will touch your heart, the location where your commitment will be the most strongly felt. Then whenever you stray from your commitment, for example, getting that extra clothing purchase you didn't need right now, you can connect back to this moment in the mirror and regain your confidence.
- **GET A MENTOR OR COACH.** One of our greatest gifts in his world is each other. Find those you know who can become your mentors and coaches. That is the point of our new Young Money University membership platform which provides members with more hands on guidance, tools and support to help you get to where you want to go.
- **IF YOU START TO SLIDE, ASK FOR A SPECIAL "EMERGENCY MEETING."** If your mentor is like most mentors he or she knows that something like this will happen. Don't wait. Get help as soon as you see your commitment is sliding. This could

look like one or two times that you find yourself sliding—
spending when those dollars were to be used for savings.

Long Term Goals

So what happens next? What does the ultimate path of a successful young person look like?

For your Long Term Goal of 10, 15, 25 or 35 from now years consider the following:

1. Save $75,000 - $100,000 in 10 years to start your dream business.
2. Save $150,000 in 15 years to pay off your home mortgage in half the time.
3. Save $1.5 – $2.5 million in 25 to 35 years through investing to retire early and work part time only because you want to work, not because you have to.

The amounts above are real snapshots of what is possible as you continue with this powerful long term financial success plan. Even with unforeseen and unexpected setbacks, you should be able to achieve these numbers with reasonable effort because of the time value of money. More on time value of money and compound interest in Chapter 4. It will blow you away.

By the time you reach a three month savings goal, you should really be proud of yourself and be locked into a long term commitment. Of course there may be times you falter. One of the most powerful things you can do is ask for help. Don't try to be brave to the detriment of your money plan. Here is a short story that might help:

> "A LITTLE BOY WAS HAVING DIFFICULTY LIFTING A HEAVY STONE.
> HIS FATHER CAME ALONG JUST THEN.
> NOTING THE BOY'S FAILURE, HE ASKED, "ARE YOU USING ALL YOUR STRENGTH?"
> "YES, I AM," THE LITTLE BOY SAID IMPATIENTLY.
> "NO, YOU'RE NOT," THE FATHER ANSWERED.
> "I AM RIGHT HERE JUST WAITING, AND YOU HAVEN'T ASKED ME TO HELP YOU."
>
> **– ANON**

As you stay steady on your path to financial success you will have the opportunity to help others and to request help. Both experiences can be very humbling and energizing at the same time.

Get Dreaming

Now that you have read this first chapter, what will you do? If you care about yourself enough, I believe you will "get dreaming." In other words, you will take what you know now, which should be different from what you knew when you started reading this chapter, and move forward.

The chapters are designed so that I can assist you as we move along one step at a time. Learn what thousands of other young adults like yourself have learned . . .that it's better to start now than to wait.

> THE FUTURE BELONGS TO THOSE WHO BELIEVE IN THE BEAUTY OF THEIR DREAMS.
>
> **– ELEANOR ROOSEVELT**

Your Action Steps

- Make A Decision To Dream. Begin to dream like never before by filling out a Dream Sheet. List both your small and big dreams/goals. Set specific financial goals (i.e....I want to own a breakfast cafe by age 30 (Big Dream/Goal) or I want to save $2,500 as a down payment on a new/used car within 12 months (Small Dream/Goal). Set materialistic goals and dream like having a certain kind of car or live in a certain type of house in the future. We all want nice things. Go for it. Then list some of your giving goals to help others along the way.

- Once you have filled this out, print out a copy and put it up where you can see it daily—your mirror in your bathroom, your refrigerator or even both.

- Begin to think about your personal WHY? Why do you ultimately want to be financially successful? Of course part of our WHY will be to have long term financial security as we get older. However, beyond financial security what else is part of your WHY? Is there something that bothers or frustrates you in our world that you want to help with? Perhaps it is third world or local hunger, human trafficking, disease, homelessness, etc.

What's Next?

I've shared with you the importance of connecting to your purpose—your WHY. Now that you are beginning to discover your dreams and aspirations, both for your finances and your life, it's time to start saving money differently. In Chapter 2, I'll help you learn why automatic saving and creating named savings account is super important and how to get started.

CHAPTER 2: STEP TWO
Save Money Automatically

Our Money Attitudes and Behaviors Tell a Story

It's amazing how much our life as a child and teenager plays into how we "turn out" in life. Researchers and data point to experiences and people (namely parents) that influenced those in prison, those who suffer from addictions of many kinds and so on. Most of the people in prison or those who suffer from addiction had tumultuous childhood experiences and/or less than engaged parents, only one less than engaged parent or no parents at all growing up.

The same goes for our experience with money as a child or teenager and how much instruction we were given by our parents or guardians to manage our money. Some of us had no instruction on how and why to save a portion of our money we earned. We just followed the attitudes and behaviors of our parents thinking later on that I will figure this money thing out on my own.

In 2008, the University of Arizona launched a longitudinal panel study of a couple of thousand students called the Arizona Pathways to Life Success for University Students. Otherwise known as the APLUS Project. This massive effort focused on collecting and studying young adults' financial knowledge, attitudes and behavior at several points over a five-year period from first year of college to post graduation in the workforce.

Examples of financial behavior in their study included paying bills on time, spending within a budget, tracking monthly expenses, saving each month, investing for long term goals and learning about finances

Some key findings of their study included the following:

- 12% of students were deemed High Functioning students given they maintained this high level of financial behavior from their first year of college to post graduation.
- 61% of students were deemed Rebounding students as they started college with moderately responsible financial behaviors, declined through college and then rebounded over their final two years of the study.
- 26% of students were deemed Struggling Students as they started college with poor financial behaviors which had further declined by year four Though their behaviors had improved two years in they were still worse than during their first year of college and significantly lower than all other participants.

According to APLUS, these findings not only suggested the benefits of responsible financial behaviors in late adolescence as a pathway to adult self-sufficiency, they also provide insight for identifying at-risk youth and designing effective interventions to promote higher functioning later in life.

Bottom line: relevant financial education and training at a young age can have a huge impact on the well-being of many people, regardless of ethnic, economic or cultural background. That is why I am so excited about this book. There is no discrimination with this 5 Step Plan. You can have a bright future with increased chances of financial security if you heed these valuable 5 Steps. You can choose this new behavior or stick with your old financial behavior. But I know you want a better future.

The Emotion of Money and Instant Gratification

It's been said so often that it feels like a cliché, but that does not make it any less true: We live in a society that values and even demands instant gratification. In so many ways we are told from a very young age that we can demand and even get anything we want immediately. Are you hungry for chicken and mashed potatoes? No problem, pop a frozen dinner in the microwave or swing through the drive-through of your local KFC, Popeyes or Chick-Fil-A and BAM! you've got it! Want to lose 20 pounds? Pop some pills that you order online, and with an upgrade to overnight shipping, you are on your way to being thin and svelte almost immediately. Unfortunately, instant gratification often gives us pleasure in the short term but does not provide true satisfaction or happiness in the long term. Sometimes eating too much of that fried chicken can give us stomach cramps in the middle of the night. No fun.

Even with this knowledge, many of us are still left with the feeling of wanting and even deserving, instant gratification. We want what we want, and we want it now. The instant gratification trap can be even more appealing to young people. We're constantly tempted by our friends that are sporting the latest smartphone, clothes or gadget. They seem to always have a fancy espresso drink from Starbuck's in their hands or never have to cook because they either eat out or order in. It's incredibly tempting to look at others and think we deserve what they have too. Suddenly, we can see that the desire for instant gratification and the feeling of entitlement that goes along with it creates some very strange and unhealthy emotions. Those emotions and desires become attached to how we deal with money.

In our consumer-driven economy, there are many other forces indoctrinating us from the time we are very young. Advertisers convince us that buying certain products can bring us happiness. They tell us that having the right clothes will attract a potential love interest, leading to the partner of our dreams. We're told that using the right cosmetics and skin care products will make us more beautiful and alluring. Every commercial, ad or television show, or movie keeps promising that elusive relationship that we think will lead to long-term happiness. We start to really believe that buying a costly drink at Starbuck's or at the local bar will somehow help us to get through the day more peacefully. While we watched Saturday morning cartoons, we took in commercials for toys and video games and fast food restaurants and breakfast cereals. All those commercials showed joyful, healthy children in happy, loving families. The featured products made the implicit promise that if we purchase the product, we too will be happy and healthy.

In some ways this desire for instant gratification and happiness through purchasing is not your fault. Most Americans have been indoctrinated from a young age to think 'buy, buy, buy' is the way to contentment. Countless forces in our culture have conditioned us to buy into the dual lie: that material goods will somehow lead to happiness and that we deserve to have whatever we want immediately. But you are an adult now, and you can choose to opt out of this lie.

Amping up Your Awareness

Understanding and having an awareness of these cultural forces helps us to begin to understand at least some of the emotion that is associated with money. We have certainly heard the proverb that money cannot buy love or happiness, but for many people the internal voice that still shouts, "If you just purchase this one product, your life will be better. You will be more attractive, more fun, and happier!" is so much louder than that old proverb. And because we all want to be attractive, fun, and most of all happy, it is simply so easy to give in to the louder, more insistent voice. Even though our heads know better, it's often difficult for our hearts to overcome the many years of conditioning, particularly the conditioning that comes from advertising. That conditioning that tells us spending money on the right product will make us happy is deeply rooted into our psyches.

Our emotions are so connected to money that it is difficult to think straight. The false promise that 'money can buy happiness' is not the only way that we are unhealthily and emotionally enmeshed with money. As a society, we too often measure an individual's success not by how happy or healthy that person is, but by how much money the person has, or at least appears to have. We see people who pursue careers which we associate with a high income: doctors, lawyers, actors, and professional athletes as truly successful. We are encouraged to get a good education so that someday we can have a high paying job, again reinforcing this idea that our success in life is somehow determined by our income. We equate cash flow with happiness and success. We begin to think that successful, happy people are big spenders. But those are just more lies that create unhealthy emotional associations with money.

Peer pressure is another factor. We want to feel like we fit in with those around us, so when we see them spending, we want to spend too. In fact, we may even feel entitled to spend whether we have the money or not! This behavior is so common that our society even has a silly cliché to refer to it: "keeping up with the Joneses." We feel entitled to have and to spend what we think our peers are spending. And if we equate spending money with success and happiness, why wouldn't we think this way? Again, our relationship with money becomes defined by lies and by feelings of entitlement and the desire for happiness that money in the end cannot possibly give.

This entire situation is made worse by the fact that so many young people simply do not have any education, training or resources to help them learn how to manage money. So they get caught up in this spiral. Another way that the emotion associated with money is crippling many people is fear. In many homes and subcultures, people are taught that it's somehow rude or crass to discuss money. For too many young people, money has become an oddly taboo subject, something their parents may have taken care of behind the scenes but did not discuss in front of the children. Yet, there is an expectation that you should somehow magically be able to manage money with no problem.

This all creates another emotion associated with money called shame. Some feel shame or embarrassment or guilt because they have been blessed with more resources than others, while other people feel the same feelings because they don't seem to have enough money. The expectation that you should know how to manage money, in spite of not having or been given the tools to do so, creates a kind of shame when you lack knowledge and mismanage money. This is wrong and not your fault.

With all the emotional associations people tend to have with earning, having, and spending money; it's no wonder so many Americans struggle with personal finance. Our judgment is clouded by these vast waves of powerful, negative emotions that we cannot think clearly, even when we do have some of the knowledge.

One obvious result of all the illogical, although understandable, and sometimes conflicting emotions that we associate with money is that many people are living outside their means. When we would do well to be saving and investing, creating a stable future for ourselves and our future families, we're spending more than we can afford on disposable goods that really provide only momentary pleasure, if even that. Far too many people even go so far as to rack up credit card debt purchasing things they don't need in the false hope that a product will bring them happiness. We will get to more on credit cards later.

Let me break it down for you; although our brains might tell us it's all a lie, for many of us our hearts still equate spending money with success and happiness. This is true for many, many people in our society, but it's especially true for young adults who don't have the tools or experience to see through the lies. So what can you do? The emotion can be so overpowering that even when people know they should save, rather than spend, they often spend anyway. How can you be a wise manager of money and bypass the emotion? Or more directly, how can you become a saver rather than a spender?

Automatic Savings: A Surefire Way to Battle Natural Temptation

The answer to pushing emotional spending to the side lies in automatic savings. And further into this chapter I will discuss how to take this a step further by creating multiple named savings accounts that will provide a wonderful "ah ha" moment for you. The concept of saving money automatically sometimes is presented as the advice to "pay yourself first." Here's the deal. When you receive a paycheck and deposit it into your checking account you need to have a portion of that check immediately go into your saving account. You do this by simply setting up an automatic transfer with from your bank or credit union's checking account into your savings account. Then, do not touch the money in your savings account, short of an emergency, but more on that later. In some ways, you want to behave as though the money in this savings account does not exist; certainly you want to behave as though dipping into it and spending it is simply not an option.

The temptation to spend money is so great that many people simply spend everything that's in their checking account, either to pay bills, by using a debit card to pay for everyday expenses, or by withdrawing cash for expenses. Most people use up every dime or dollar that they have access to. In order to save, you must move your money *automatically* out of the way of this temptation. You can tell your bank or credit union by visiting the branch or even doing this online to take out a certain amount of money on a specific day of the month like the 5th, 15th or 25th. Monthly saving automation is huge for your short term and long term financial health and success.

In the last chapter, I encouraged you to dream small and big and come up with financial and personal goals. Starting to save now, even if your income is small, is the first step towards reaching many goals and living out your dreams.

Become a Saver

Your "Money Engine" = checking account

As I have said before, you must open up a checking and savings account if you want to follow the Young Money Plan 5 Step Plan for yourself. Neither account should cost you anything. If there is a monthly fee for your checking account just go to another bank or credit union. There are plenty that have no fee.

Let's face it; a checking account is not very sexy or exciting. In fact, for some of you who already have a checking account, it represents some pain because checking accounts are primarily used to pay bills. However, I want you to begin to think differently about your checking account going forward.

Your checking account should now be viewed as your "money engine;" the piece that is moving you forward, day-to-day. There are two important pieces of this analogy. An engine keeps things going and an engine is non-personal and emotionless. Treating your checking account as an engine allows you to save and spend wisely. It also helps you remove the troubling emotions that are too often associated with money. In Chapter 4, I will show you how your checking account (your money engine) can help you create significant wealth over time!

We will talk more about budgeting later, but you should know right now that the source of your monthly budget is your checking account. You will use your checking account to pay for day-to-day expenses and regular bills. In this way, your checking account continues to function like an engine, allowing you to chug forward each day.

Most employers offer, and some even require, direct deposit of paychecks for their employees. What this means is that instead of having a physical paycheck handed to you that you must then deposit in the bank, on your payday funds are automatically transferred right into your account. If you are not currently using direct deposit for your paycheck, I strongly recommend that you do so right away. This saves you the hassle of having to make a trip to the bank to deposit a check

For many of you that are not working a steady job because you are a full time student but you still have some monthly income; you can still set up monthly automatic savings with your bank or credit union. Even if your transfer is only $10. The amount of your first automatic transfer to savings is not the point here. It's that you are now creating an *automatic savings habit*. And this is big. As you begin to earn more income you simply increase your monthly automatic savings.

Your "Life Happens" Account = Savings Account

While your checking account may be thought of as your "money engine," your savings account is for all the moments that you can't predict. It's your "life happens" account. Let me tell you what I mean by this.

You can put together a monthly cash flow plan (budget) for all of your expenses and anticipate these fairly accurately such as food, clothing, utilities, car payment, gas, cell phone, etc. Again, we will talk about this more in chapter 3. But what do you do when unexpected things come up that you simply hadn't planned for? Your car needs repairs. You need to cough up money for a speeding or parking ticket. You shattered your iPhone or Galaxy screen. Your refrigerator dies. How do you pay for the life events that your monthly budget just doesn't cover? If you're like far too many Americans, you may be tempted to pay for these events with a credit card. Believe me, it's easy to justify the use of a credit card when you tell yourself, "Well, I've tried to be thoughtful about spending money, but hey, life happens."

Your savings account, rather than using high interest credit cards, should be the first place you turn when life happens to you. This is why I call it the your "life happens" account. Or what most people call an Emergency Fund. When your car needs new tires, belts or a radiator or you are issued a traffic ticket, you'll hopefully have most if not all of the money set aside. Sometimes we're tempted to think we don't need to save because our lives run smooth. Let me reassure you, no matter your age, life will happen to you sooner rather than later, if it hasn't already. When it does, you will be thankful for your "life happens" emergency fund.

Create Multiple Named Savings Accounts

Now if you really want to create an enhanced sense of financial peace in your life check with your bank or credit union to see if they offer multiple savings accounts or sometimes called sub accounts or share accounts at credit unions, that you can name. For example, you can name one savings account "Car Expense" that is for all future car maintenance and repairs. Another could be named "Future Car" whereby the money automatically saved per month in this account is for the purchase of your first or next car. You could name other savings accounts "Giving", "Travel", "Clothes", "School", "Shoes" or whatever you want. The big picture here is that when you save money automatically per month into multiple named savings accounts this allows you to have the money in hand when your car inevitably needs repairs or you have the desire to buy some new jeans, shoes and that cool shirt. Financial stress is lessened as a result of this monthly automatic savings habit happening within multiple named accounts.

The other benefit of named savings accounts is that it deters you from free spirited spending. When you put a *name to nearly every dollar you earn* it's much more difficult to spend freely which we know leads to regret and stress down the road. Think about it. What's the chance that you would take money out of your "Future Car" savings account to pay for a fleeting thought to purchase a new pair of designer jeans you saw while in the mall? Naming nearly every dollar keeps you focused on your WHY and your financial goals at the same time. I'm a huge fan of multiple named savings accounts! And so are thousands of other millennials that are now saving money this way.

Before Snapshot

Jonathan Prata, although only 18 years old, will soon be a junior at the Florida International University. He recently graduated with an Associate's degree from Miami Dade College in Miami, Florida. Before attending Young Money LIVE! Jonathan had some sense of setting aside money in savings.

"My parents simply told me to start working when I turned 16," says Jonathan, "and that I should be sure to save some money. But they didn't really tell me *how* to go about saving, and I knew almost nothing about saving and growing money."

Jonathan began doing work around the house and odd jobs here and there, but he was, to use his own words "a random saver." "I did open a checking and even a savings account in high school and I did have a debit card", says Jonathan. When I would work, I would put some of the money into my savings account, but I also had a money box at home where I would store random cash. I'd use this as spending money and also put some into my checking account so that I could use my debit card. I really had no system, and in the end my savings account had almost nothing in it."

Saving money wasn't a priority for Jonathan. He simply didn't know any better. He wasn't exactly living outside his means, but he certainly wasn't saving anything towards his "life happens" account or any other names savings accounts that were mentioned earlier.

After Snapshot

"After attending Young Money LIVE!, Step 2 really hit home for me, says Jonathan. I realized I hadn't been saving at all. For as long as I've been earning money, I've been spending it freely, and it caught up to me." Jonathan says that now that he understands the importance of not just saving but automatic saving, he's excited to put this step into action. By having his checking and savings account, now it's simply a matter of him setting up an automatic transfer each month from his checking to savings accounts.

Jonathan says, "I know that being financially successful isn't always easy, but I know that this plan will help me quite a bit. And the steps I need to take are straightforward and manageable." Jonathan is on his way to financial success. He has identified some financial and life dreams, and he's ready to put Step 2 into action and set up automatic savings.

Step Two Action Steps

- Become aware of the various ways that emotions are connected to how you approach money. Realize that many of these emotions come from lies that our culture has fed you whether you're conscious of them or not.
- Reflect on your own money attitudes and behaviors as a child or in your teen years. Did you spend everything you earned or was given as a gift? Were you encouraged to save money? What negative influences about money did you have growing up?

- If you have not done so already, open up a checking and savings account at a traditional bank, an online bank, or a credit union. Make sure they offer multiple savings accounts that you can name.
- Once your accounts are set up, create an automatic monthly transfer from your checking to at least one savings account.
- Base your monthly cash flow plan (budget) on what is in your checking account only. Don't use savings for monthly living expenses. Your savings account(s) are your "life happens" accounts to be used for emergencies, unplanned and planned expenses All with a name to each of these future expenses and spending goals.

Now that you have set up your checking and savings accounts and have begun saving automation, what do you do next to create some more financial security? Step Three of the Young Money Plan includes thoughtful spending and the practice of setting up and sticking to a monthly cash flow plan (budget). The bottom line is that your financial health is based on self-control and the ability to say "no sometimes"

There are many online, national, regional, or local banks and credit unions that can get you set up on Step 2 to create automatic savings within your new named savings accounts. A few that I like include the following.

Capital One 360 (capitalone360.com)

One of my favorite online banks. With your checking account, you receive a debit card, you can make mobile deposits, and you have access to over 36,000 fee free ATM"s and 2,000 Capital One ATM's. You can have multiple savings accounts and create a nickname for each of them. This enables you to automatically save per month into multiple named savings accounts, which will really keep you on track financially.

PNC Bank - Virtual Wallet (pnc.com/virtual-wallet)

Virtual Wallet from PNC Bank provides you with three accounts. Your Spend account is your checking account which comes with a debit card and access to over 7,200 ATM's to withdraw money with no fee Your Reserve account is for short term savings and your Growth account is for long term savings for larger purchases down the road.

Ally Bank (ally.com)

Another favorite online bank, Ally Bank offers mobile savings and checking accounts with above average interest rates; not that today's interest rates on savings or checking will make you rich soon. Ally Bank has mobile check deposit, no minimum deposit required and no monthly maintenance fees.

Credit Unions

Your local credit union can also help you with Step 2 and setting up automatic savings. Many young people are not aware that credit unions are a financial institution just like a bank. Credit unions have been around for several decades and their numbers keep growing. The major difference between a bank and a credit union is that when you join a credit union you become a member/owner and credit unions are designated non-profit organizations. Credit unions also see themselves as different from mainstream banks with a mission to be community oriented, to serve people and not focused solely on profit.

Over the last several years, credit unions have been doing a good job of offering younger consumers relevant banking products and services including online and mobile banking, bill pay, and person-to-person payments. Recently credit unions have created a shared network of branches and ATM's that allow members to do their banking in nearly all 50 states with little to no fees.

CHAPTER 3: STEP THREE
Just Say No Sometimes

As Will Smith once said, "Too many people spend money they haven't earned to buy things they don't want, to impress people they don't like." In the last chapter, I explained why you should have, at a minimum, a checking and a savings account. Having multiple named savings accounts to deal with a variety of "life Happens" expenses and events is even better to get you on a road to real financial health and success. Once your accounts are set up and ready to go, what is the next step? Your next step is to set up a monthly cash flow plan, otherwise known as a spending plan or budget.

By the way, most people I talk to like the words "cash flow plan" instead of budget so this is what I like to call it. Bottom line is they are one in the same. This monthly cash flow plan will enable you to say no sometimes to things that you may want but ultimately don't need.

Needs vs. Wants

Let's begin by covering the difference between needs and wants. This distinction is important because many people run into money difficulty by not distinguishing between the two.

Now, of course, you know the difference: a need is something that is essential to your survival, something that we all require in order to live in a healthy fashion, while a want is something that you can live equally as well without. It's really that simple. The problem is that many people do not stop and think about this difference before making a purchase. The truth is that our needs, as opposed to wants, make up a pretty short list: food, water, basic clothing, a place to live and health care. Of course, humans have other needs—love, friendship—that money truly cannot buy.

Additionally, you should consider that while you have legitimate needs--food, clothing, and shelter--you can generally choose to meet these needs in ways that make either more or less economic sense. For example, you may honestly need a new pair of jeans. Maybe the holes you have in them are not the kind of holes that you see from some high fashion jeans. So it's time to move on. This does not, however, mean that you need a pair of expensive designer jeans at this early state of your life. Some designer jeans can cost between $150 - $350 in upscale stores, as compared to jeans from, say Old Navy which cost about $35.00 or 20% of the cost of upscale designer jeans. So do you need jeans? Yes! Do you need to spend nearly $200.00 on jeans? Absolutely not!

Now, am I saying that you are only allowed to spend money on needs and not spend anything on wants? Of course not. But realizing what you truly need now is a first step towards saying no sometimes to things that you don't need. It's also a way to begin to think about creating your monthly cash flow plan, for this will prioritize where and how you spend money, realizing that you pay for needs before wants.

Let's not forget Step 1 in Chapter 1. It's the foundation to achieve financial success. As you begin to define and cultivate your personal WHY and write out your short, mid-term and long term goals it will become easier to say no sometimes to your wants for now. Because you have a financial plan that you truly desire to follow. I love what Dave Ramsay says about short term sacrifice. "Live like no one else now so you can live like no one else later". This is truth.

Awareness – Jeff, John, Chelsey and Shareen

Have you ever reached the end of a month or a pay cycle, with your paycheck still five days away but with no money in your account? Maybe you tried to use your ATM card to pay for something and had the uncomfortable experience of being told by the store clerk that your card was declined. You probably wondered where all the money had gone.

It felt like your paycheck went into the account one day, and that felt great, knowing all that money was there for you to spend. But now you feel panicked, not knowing how you are going to get through the next few days. Where did all the money go? You know you haven't made any big purchases, so how could your entire paycheck have evaporated before the next one came in? One sad reality is that many people are not even aware of what they spend all their money on each week, month or pay period. If this is you don't worry about it. Today is a new day and you're now going to be have hyper awareness for the benefit of reaching your life dreams and goals

It's important that you know where your money is going—this allows you to begin to control your money, rather than being controlled by it. I recommend that you begin by tracking everything, yes *everything*, that you spend for a week and then for a month. This tracking of every penny spent will give you an overview of where the money is going in a particular month. It's a kind of pre-budget step that will allow a starting point from which to build a realistic monthly cash flow plan, one that acknowledges what you spend.

Putting together a cash flow plan and then sticking to it does several important things for you. First, it creates an awareness of where your money is going each month. You will know what you're spending money on. You will not end up in the position of being five days away from your next paycheck and having nothing in your account, because you've allotted money to last for the entire month. Because you have taken the time to think about and create a monthly cash flow plan, you're thinking about money logically and differently than most people. You're also removing some of the difficult emotions that we attach to money. This helps you to say no to what might feel like a "need" in the moment, but is really just a "want."

When I get to this step (Step 3) at our YOUNG MONEY LIVE! events, I always ask people in the audience to tell me what their biggest spending vice or vices are. In other words, what is it that you spend a lot of money on every month that you really know is a want vs a need. During a recent stop on the campus of the University of Maryland, a student named Jeff quickly spoke up and said "Chipotle." Much laughter and head nodding in agreement came from other young people in the crowd as they too felt that Chipotle was one of the culprits where they spend a lot of money on a regular basis. Jeff went so far to tell me and the rest of the audience that he visits Chipotle 5-7 times a week. Yes, he said PER WEEK. I loved Jeff's honesty. He was tracking with me throughout the presentation and it was very clear that he wanted to get ahead with money and learn a real plan or system to help him save and spend his money better. More importantly than just saving and spending money – Jeff noted that he is doing this plan to accomplish and reach some goals and dreams for his life.

John attended one of our events at Towson University and shouted that he spends way too much money on alcohol and acknowledged this is one of his spending vices. You don't need me to tell you that this can lead to a much bigger issue than just financial. Once again, I admired John's honesty and his desire to get moving on managing his money better so he can pursue much bigger goals and dreams for his life.

Like Chipotle, another favorite spending vice for many young people is Starbucks or the local coffee house near campus. Chelsey was one of many students who raised their hands and admitted they "need" to have their daily gourmet coffee on the way to school or work. But for Chelsey, she said Starbucks was a daily ritual and a friend next to her jokingly said aloud "she has a Starbucks issue". We all laughed. Then I discussed how one of Chelsey's "just say no sometimes" action steps will be her brewing her own coffee (even using Starbucks coffee beans) at home a couple of times a week to save a decent chunk of money every month. She agreed because of what she heard about Step 1.

No matter what group of millennials I speak to, nearly all spending vices are categorized into three categories: food, entertainment, and appearance. For women, most overspending they have told me is in fashion/clothing, movies, skin care, and food. On the other hand, men's spending vices are predominantly food, gaming, alcohol, music, and, to a lesser extent, clothes.

You probably remember Shareen from Chapter 1. She quickly pointed out to me that fashion was her biggest spending vice and the primary source of her overspending prior to hearing me speak. It was so much fun to hear her tell me a couple of months later how she has dismissed staying up with fashion and only buying clothes and accessories that are in her newly made cash flow plan. The simple change in her financial behavior is because of the small and big goals she has written down while flushing out her personal WHY.

Financial Stress Caused by Overindulgence

Nearly 75% of the hands go up at a Young Money LIVE! event when I ask young people if they have spent money on something in the last month in which they have felt regret. Amazing right? I'm sure you have experienced this same "purchase regret" too. I certainly have. But don't fret. You're becoming aware of what your behavior is now in order to make changes because you have a renewed motivation – YOUR WHY.

So what do you do when you're simply out of money? If you're like many Americans, you use a credit card. This is certainly a tempting option. I mean, there you are with several days of truly needing to eat, although you have nothing in your account. And so you go to the grocery store and pay with a credit card. You

adds up

probably even justify it by telling yourself that food is a need, not a want. But then what happens is this: Let's say you spend $50.00 at the grocery store, which is quite a low figure to feed a person for three meals a day, for several days. But that is $50.00 that you'll need to pay the next month, and $50.00 less that you have to go towards the next month's budget.

Now, I'm assuming that if you ran out of money five days before a paycheck, your money is tight each month. You probably cannot really afford to take $50.00 out of your next month's budget. In fact, if you don't change your habits, a $50.00 shortfall one month could become a $100.00 shortfall the next. You can see how this quickly becomes a self-perpetuating cycle.

Now, if your money is tight and if you haven't budgeted for it, you may not be able to pay off the $50.00 credit card statement when it arrives. As a result, you merely make the minimum payment, maybe $15.00. This will leave you with a shortfall of $65.00 the next month, assuming that your spending habits are the same. So you charge groceries for $65.00, bringing your credit card balance to just over $100.00. If you continue with this cycle of charging, even relatively small amounts, and paying only the minimum, you quickly rack up credit card debt. Instant gratification creates a cycle of budget shortfall and financial stress.

It gets worse. If you make only the minimum payment, that charge of $50.00 will take you four months to clear. But a charge of $100.00 will take eight months to pay off, making only a minimum payment. This quickly adds up—you are creating a cycle in which you will be in debt for months, all because of poor planning and giving in to the desire for instant gratification.

Once started, this cycle is difficult to break. It goes on and on, creating a prolonged state of financial stress.

Because so many emotions are tied to money, financial stress also means emotional stress. Charging $50.00, then $65.00 in the above scenario means that you are creating a situation in which you will have to worry about money for the next 8 months. It means eight months of emotional debt, rather than eight months of control and freedom.

You Inc!

How you stop this cycle overspending is to create and stick to a monthly cash flow plan by looking at yourself as your own business. Young people really resonate with this as there is much interest among today's youth to start a business someday. So for now I want you to call yourself YOU INC! For example, if I was still single I would create a budget called Todd Romer, Inc.

Like any business, you hope to be profitable or have a net income right? So by looking at your monthly revenue minus your monthly expenses, you can quickly see how YOU, Inc. is doing and what adjustments you need to make to make in order to at least break even or make a "profit." This will make creating your cash flow plan (budget) more fun and enjoyable.

So let's start with the basic elements of your cash flow plan.
1. Know your monthly revenue. Wages and tips from jobs or any bonuses.
2. Know your monthly expenses by writing down your fixed and variable expenses.

Fixed expenses typically include:

- Housing (rent or mortgage)
- Utilities (mobile phone, internet, tv/cable, water, electric, gas, trash)
- Savings (your life happens account)
- Emergency Fund (for the truly unexpected like a job loss)
- Investment Fund (see Chapter 4)
- Insurance (car, health, life, disability)
- Giving (see chapter 5)

Variable expenses typically include:

- Transportation (car payment, gas, tolls, maintenance)
- Food (grocery and eating out)
- Clothing
- Entertainment (movies, sports, gaming, etc.)
- Housing maintenance (if you have a mortgage)

Because many of you reading this book are between age 18-29 you have a wonderful, ironclad template to build a solid financial future. When you treat your fixed expenses as non-negotiable line items, you are set up well to deal with the normal life happens expenses that will inevitably happen to you, me and all of us.

Many of you may be living at home while working or some of you may be in school with many of these expenses being paid by your parents or guardians. So you have a great head start to follow your own monthly cash flow plan now and learn about additional real life's expenses when you are living on your own in the near future.

Young Money 5 Step Plan Action Steps

- Start today by tracking your spending. Record everything you spend for at least two weeks, then a month. It's as easy as snapping a cellphone photo of every receipt you get, when you get it. This will give you a picture (literally) of where you are currently spending money. Or you can write down your daily spending in your notes area of your cell phone or in a small notebook you carry with you or in your car. This creates awareness which is a huge first step when preparing to create your new monthly cash flow plan.

- Identify the difference between needs and wants. Before making any purchase, ask yourself whether it is a need or a want. Remember, needs are things you have to have to survive (food, water, housing, transportation, clothing) and wants are things you'd really like to have, but can survive without (just released video games, eating out instead of cooking at home, entertainment, sporting gear).

- Write out a potential cash flow plan to implement next month and remember the You Inc. mindset of how you want your "own business" to go each month.

CHAPTER 4: STEP FOUR
Get Into the Game of Investing Automatically

This chapter is the real game changer for your life. By understanding investing it can have a profound impact on the goals and dreams that you're beginning to set for yourself. Once you begin to say "no sometimes" to your immediate wants and you begin to have a surplus each month, what can you do with your money to make it grow?

After setting aside a sufficient amount in your multiple named savings accounts or your "life happens" accounts, it's important to turn your attention to investing. Simply put, investing is a way to make your money multiply, even exponentially, over time. This is how true financial wealth is accomplished. Some people feel intimidated by the idea of investing, but this is really only because they don't have the information to allow them to make informed choices. Investing is where the real fun happens, and you can enjoy the experience of watching your money grow. In fact, this is my favorite step of the Young Money 5 Step Plan because it will impact all the other four steps in a significant way. Understanding the power of investing at a young age can significantly impact your dreaming, your WHY, irrational spending and how much you can help others during your life's journey in dramatic fashion.

For clarification, investing I speak of in this book is primarily in stocks of publicly traded companies like Apple, Coca Cola, Procter and Gamble, IBM, Microsoft etc. There are many other forms of investments that make sense and can create long term wealth such as real estate but I am referring to the ease and opportunity that exists within the U.S. stock market. Shortly you will learn more about the history of the stock market but let's first learn how invested money works to your advantage.

The Time Value of Money

The value of money changes over time. Has your grandmother or grandfather ever told you that the soda you purchased for $1.50 from a vending machine or fast food restaurant he purchased for $.15 when he was your age? Currently, the median price for a single family home is just over $200,000.00.[8] Whereas in 1942, the average home price was under $4,000.00.[9] From these examples, you can see that the amount that a dollar can purchase tends to decrease quite a lot over time.

While the amount that a dollar can purchase has decreased over time, people are not necessarily experiencing a lower standard of living as a result. This is due to what we call inflation—as time goes on and due to a variety of factors, prices rise. In a healthy economy, this is offset by a rise in wages. In other words, although things tend to rise in cost over time, people also tend to make more over time, allowing them to be able to purchase about the same amount of goods that they were able to in the past, although at a higher cost. However, today there is much data that suggest wages have not caught up nearly enough with the rise in cost of goods and services.

But here's the takeaway for you; simply putting money away— hiding it under your mattress the way some people used to do— does nothing to increase the value of your money. If you simply squirrel money away for the future, you'll actually be buying less with that money because of inflation. Today, most banks and credit unions are paying less than 1% interest in a savings account so as I mentioned before, you will not create wealth in your savings account. For many decades prior to 1995 you could argue that a savings account could create great wealth as it was paying interest of 5-7% annually. Not anymore.

So how can you save money and actually encourage it to grow and be worth more? Let me introduce you to the concept of compound interest. Compound interest is your friend. In fact, Albert Einstein described compound interest as the "eighth wonder of the world". He who understands it earns it; he who doesn't pays it." This nearly magical concept assures that the dollar you save and invest today will multiply over time and allow you even more purchasing power in the future than that dollar has today.

Compound Interest Is Your Friend

Compound interest simply means that any profits an investor makes from an investment are then reinvested. This allows your money to grow exponentially over time. Say, for example, that you invest $500.00 initially. If in the first year you earn a 10% return on that investment, or $50.00, your investment would be worth $550.00. Now if you did not touch that money and were to also earn a 10% return in the second year, you'd earn a new profit of $55.00. In just two years, then, your investment of $500.00 would have grown to $605.00. Ideally, you will want to continue reinvesting every year. Over time, then, you earn interest (money) not just on your initial investment of $500.00, but also on the interest you earn year after year. This earning of interest upon interest you have already earned is called compound interest.

It's compound interest that really allows your money to multiply. As an example, an initial investment of $50,000.00 with an annual return of 11% would grow to over $1,000,000.00 in 30 years. And that's *without* adding any money to the initial investment but simply reinvesting any interest or earnings.[10]

The way that compound interest works its best magic, however, is over time. This means that it's best to begin investing and reinvesting any profit as early in your life as possible. In fact, if you start investing early, through the magic of compound interest, you can earn much more money than if you were to wait and invest larger amounts.

For example, let's look at a comparison of investing now versus waiting with chart on the next page. Julia decides to invest $250 per month or $3,000 beginning at the age of 19. She invests the same amount every month through the age of 26. Julia then stops investing all together. Her total investment during those eight years was $24,000. Assuming a 10% annual rate of return on her investments, she ends up with $1,552,739.00. Over $1.5 million! Sounds good, right? It absolutely should and it is real because the average rate of return in the stock market over the last 100 years has been just over 10%.

	Julia Investing at Age 19 (Assuming 10% Annual Return)		Stephen Investing at Age 27 (Assuming 10% Annual Return)	
AGE	INVEST $3,000/YEAR		INVEST $3,000/YEAR	
19	$3,000	$3,300	-	-
20	$3,000	$6,930	-	-
21	$3,000	$10,923	-	-
22	$3,000	$15,315	-	-
23	$3,000	$20,146	-	-
24	$3,000	$25,461	-	-
25	$3,000	$31,307	-	-
26	$3,000	$37,738	-	-
27	$0	$41,512	$3,000	$3,300
28	$0	$45,663	$3,000	$6,930
29	$0	$50,229	$3,000	$10,923
30	$0	$55,252	$3,000	$15,315
31	$0	$60,778	$3,000	$20,146
32	$0	$66,855	$3,000	$25,461
33	$0	$73,541	$3,000	$31,307
34	$0	$80,895	$3,000	$37,738
35	$0	$88,985	$3,000	$44,812
36	$0	$97,883	$3,000	$52,593
37	$0	$107,672	$3,000	$61,152
38	$0	$118,439	$3,000	$70,568
39	$0	$130,283	$3,000	$80,924
40	$0	$143,311	$3,000	$92,317
41	$0	$157,642	$3,000	$104,849
42	$0	$173,407	$3,000	$118,634
43	$0	$190,747	$3,000	$133,797
44	$0	$209,822	$3,000	$150,477
45	$0	$230,804	$3,000	$168,825
46	$0	$253,885	$3,000	$189,007
47	$0	$279,273	$3,000	$211,208
48	$0	$307,201	$3,000	$235,629
49	$0	$337,921	$3,000	$262,491
50	$0	$371,713	$3,000	$292,041
51	$0	$408,884	$3,000	$324,545
52	$0	$449,773	$3,000	$360,299
53	$0	$494,750	$3,000	$399,629
54	$0	$544,225	$3,000	$442,892
55	$0	$598,648	$3,000	$490,482
56	$0	$658,513	$3,000	$542,830
57	$0	$724,364	$3,000	$600,413
58	$0	$796,800	$3,000	$663,754
59	$0	$876,480	$3,000	$733,430
60	$0	$964,128	$3,000	$810,073
61	$0	$1,060,541	$3,000	$894,380
62	$0	$1,166,596	$3,000	$987,118
63	$0	$1,288,255	$3,000	$1,089,130
64	$0	$1,411,581	$3,000	$1,201,343
65	$0	$1,552,739	$3,000	$1,324,777

Listen closely. Despite all the ups and downs in the stock market throughout the years including the Great Depression in the 1920's, all of the world wars, many geopolitical events, America's own economic crisis in 2007, etc the stock market still has returned to investors, on average, over 10% per year.

Now, let's look at the chart again and see how Stephen turned out with his investment. Stephen waited until he was 27 to begin investing $250 per month or $3,000 per year. Unlike Julia, Stephen invested every month until the age of 65. His total investment was $117,000 or nearly five times the amount that Julia invested and through compounding his investment amounted to $1,324,777. Despite that Stephen invested more than Julia by a large sum he has nearly $225,000 less than Julia. Crazy right?

I use this example when I present the Young Money 5 Step Plan to audiences of 10 to 1,000. And I see jaws drop all the time. Here is the real kicker. If you are Julia in the example, you are not going to stop investing when you reach age 27. Why would you? And for most people, as they earn more income per year in their jobs or their own businesses, they can invest more than $250 per month. So the numbers can reach into the many millions by the time your reach age 65!

I hope you see the dramatic impact of compound interest and the time value of money. Compound interest can be your best ally in creating financial health and wealth, but it works best if you begin investing early. I believe that you cannot afford not to invest given the power behind compound interest. And it is easier today to invest than any generation before you; and with very little money to start. I will give you my recommendations of a few investment companies to begin investing in a moment, but before I tell you, let's take a quick look at the history of the stock market in western culture.

A Brief History of the Stock Market

The "Stock Market" is certainly a term we have all heard, but most young adults, in fact most Americans, really do not know much about what these two words mean. If you are in this group, then, you certainly are not alone. So what *is* the stock market? A way to begin answering this important question is to take a look at a brief history of how the market developed. In the United States, when most people use the term the "stock market," they mean the New York Stock Exchange, or NYSE, says Andrew Beattie in his article "The Birth of Stock Exchanges."[11] But the NYSE developed from a much older tradition that comes from Western Europe. In Venice, as early as the 1300s and in Belgium as early as the 1530s, brokers, and money lenders would issue promissory notes and bonds for debts, even government debts.[12] Although these financial products are technically not stocks, these transactions led to the birth of the modern stock exchange.

According to Beattie, the first stocks developed in the 1600s, as many British, French, and Dutch companies began trading in the East Indies and Asia. Merchant ships sailing from these countries faced significant threats from pirates and weather, and in order to reduce the threat that any one merchant may face from the potential loss of his ships, merchants began seeking investors.[13] Basically, investors would "put up money for the voyage—outfitting the ship and crew in return for a percentage of the proceeds if the voyage was successful," according to

Beattie.[14] But as the various East India Companies were formed, investors began to put their money not towards a particular ship or voyage but into a particular company, one that would undertake a number of voyages.[15] When these companies would make a profit, that money would be divided among those who had invested in the company, with the dividends being allotted according to the amount that an individual had originally invested. In essence then, the investors become part owners in the company and put up money in hopes of profiting from the company's success. These East India Companies then became "the first modern joint stock companies," argues Beattie.[16] And here we have the real birth of the modern concept of stock.

This tells you something about what stocks actually are; they are small shares of ownership in a company, which investors can purchase. Investors do so with the intention of having a share in the profits of the company. Most investors put money into a variety of organizations in order to reduce risk. Basically, an investor does not want to put all of his money into just one company because should that organization fail, he would lose everything. Just like you have heard the saying, "don't put all of your eggs in one basket." Instead, investors spread their money around as a way to reduce risk. This is a practice called diversification.

The New York Stock Exchange was formed in 1817; 19 years after the first stock exchange was formed in London. Although not the first stock exchange in the United States, the NYSE quickly became the most powerful.[17] Located on Wall Street in New York City, the name of the street quickly became synonymous with American financial activity and markets. According to Beattie, London's stock exchange became the most powerful in Europe. And eventually, many other nations from around the world took notice and studied both the London and the NYSE and opened their own exchanges.[18]

The NYSE has faced many ups and downs over the decades, with the most notable being the crash of October 1929, leading to the Great Depression. Currently, the NYSE's biggest competitor is the NASDAQ, a different style of stock exchange that "does not inhabit a physical space" but "instead is a network of computers that execute trades electronically."[19] Currently, although the NASDAQ lists more companies than the NYSE, the NYSE is still the larger, more powerful market, holding more shares and trading more money than the NASDAQ.[20]

Now that you understand the history behind the development of the stock market, it is important that you distinguish between the various types of options and financial products that are available via the stock market. The most basic of these are simply stocks.

What Are Stocks?

As discussed before, stocks are a portion of ownership in a company. Purchasing stock in a company, then, means buying a partial share of ownership and putting money towards a company's endeavors. Owning stock in a company also means sharing in a company's financial success. The financial success that a company enjoys is shared with stockholders or shareholders in payments called dividends. Often, investors choose to reinvest these dividends back into the company.

There are two different types of stocks: common stocks and preferred stocks.[21] Common stockholders typically have the right to vote about the future of a company at regular investors' meetings, while receiving dividends from the success of a company. Preferred stockholders generally do not have voting privileges, but receive larger dividends than common stockholders.[22] Stocks are the basic building block of most investment portfolios. Historically, stocks have performed very well over time as compared to other investments.[23]

What Are Bonds?

Another type of investment is the bond. When you purchase a bond, you are basically loaning money to either a company or a government entity. When companies or municipalities, including state and national governments, issue bonds, they are basically raising funds by asking a number of people to make small loans towards a particular goal.

These bonds are then paid back to the individual investors, with interest, at a stipulated period of time. Bonds are generally lower risk than stocks, but this also means that the payoff tends to be lower as well. In this sense, bonds are a "safer" investment than stocks. You know ahead of time what amount you will be getting in return and what the timeframe is for the return on your investment. Most investment professionals suggest owning more bonds than stocks as you near retirement and beyond simply because of less risk associated with bonds.

What Are Mutual Funds?

Mutual funds are made up of a "pool of funds collected from many investors for the purpose of investing in securities such as stocks, bonds, money market instruments and similar assets."[24] Professional money managers oversee and operate mutual funds.

An advantage of mutual funds over some other investment tools is that investors with relatively small amounts of capital can buy into a larger pool and thus be able to invest in "diversified portfolios of stocks, bonds and other securities, which would be quite difficult, if not impossible, to create with a small amount of capital."[25] The profit or loss any one investor experiences is proportional to the amount the investor has put into the fund.

Some mutual funds are guided by particular mission statements or interests. For example, some are dedicated strictly to investing in eco-friendly companies and programs. Some investors like this type of mutual fund because they are able to invest in a way that is guided by their values and conscience. There are also mutual funds that invest in certain sectors like technology, healthcare, energy or overseas economies.

What are Index Funds?

Index funds are a type of mutual fund that has a portfolio of stocks or bonds that mimics and tracks the components of a market index, such as the Standard & Poor's 500 Index (S&P 500). An index mutual fund is said to give broad market exposure, low operating costs and low portfolio turnover. Warren Buffet, known as the one of the best investors of all time and one of the wealthiest people in the world, is a fan of index funds because of their low cost and how it is a passive way to invest.

What Are Exchange Traded Funds?

Exchange traded funds, or ETFs, are a relatively new investment product. They function like mutual funds and index funds in many ways: they are built of a variety of stocks and other investment tools, thus creating a diversified portfolio for a relatively small amount of money. Also, like mutual funds, ETFs are managed by professional investment managers. An ETF however, "trades like an individual stock" [26] which means that "ETFs offer you the same intraday pricing you get when trading stocks and bonds through a broker on a major stock exchange." [27]

According to Vanguard, a prominent investment firm, ETFs have some distinct advantages over mutual funds. ETFs offer a lower minimum initial investment and lower costs overall.[28] In general, ETFs tend to be more "tax-efficient," which may mean that you save on taxes, as compared to mutual funds.[29] Additionally, the fact that ETFs can be traded in the same way as stocks translates into greater flexibility for the investor.[30]

The flexibility and especially the relatively low requirements for an initial investment make ETFs a particularly good choice for young investors.

Automatic Investing is the Key

Quite simply, automatic investing means choosing to invest a specific, predetermined dollar amount during a particular period, most likely each month or every pay period. This is similar to when I discussed automatically allocating part of each paycheck to your new named savings accounts. Likewise, you can arrange through an investment firm to have a predetermined amount automatically deducted from your checking account each month and invested into any one of the investment choices I discussed above. How cool is that! I highly recommend that not only do you invest a predetermined amount each month but that you simply let any stock appreciation or dividend payout from your investment sit or get reinvested, so that you can benefit from compound interest, as discussed above. Automation combined with letting compound interest do its thing is the key to creating wealth over time.

What Are Dividends?

As I just mentioned the word "dividend' in the previous paragraph I want to make sure you know exactly what a dividend is. While not all publicly traded companies issue a dividend to investors many certainly do. So when a company earns a profit they pay out to shareholders a portion of those profits which is called a dividend. Think about this for a moment. If you have a company that earns a profit every year and you own their stock you would get paid a dividend of perhaps 1-4% just for owning their stock. We are not talking about any stock price appreciation. Let's take Microsoft for example. As of the writing of this book they pay an annual dividend rate of 2.6%. So, if the stock never moves higher after you bought it during a one year period you will still have earned a 2.6% return on your money. That dividend yield alone is 15x more than what a bank savings account is paying in interest. So reinvesting any dividends paid out by companies in your mutual fund, index fund or ETF is important to long term wealth creation due to compounding.

How Risk is Reduced through Automatic Investing

One really helpful thing about automatic investing is that it actually works to reduce your risk of losing money. Through a strategy called *dollar-cost averaging*, you are able to purchase more shares of stock through your mutual fund, index fund or exchange traded fund when share prices are low and fewer when prices are high. Let me explain further because this is a very big deal. You don't have to be an expert in the stock market to know that stocks go up and down every day and have done so for the last 100 plus years. Nobody, including Warren Buffet, who is considered one of the most savvy stock investors of all time, knows what stocks will do on any given day. Nobody can perfectly time the stock market by buying stocks at their lowest and selling when stocks are at their highest. By dollar cost averaging and investing money automatically every month (or 12 times per year), you will buy into the stock market at a low point some months and other months when it is high. The bottom line is that you really don't care what stock prices are doing because you are investing every month to build wealth over time.

As discussed previously, over the last 100 plus years the stock market as a whole has provided investors with an average annual rate of return of more than 10 percent. This is the reason you are investing automatically per month to create true financial wealth over time by letting compound interest do its magic. Another example: if you invested $100 per month with an 11% annual return, you would have $159,058 after 25 years. Your total investment during those 25 years was $30,000. In 40 years after a total investment of $48,000, you would have $867,896! And by the way those numbers get into the millions as you invest more per month, which is very easy to do through your company's 401(k) retirement plan. See Action Steps at the end of this chapter for more information on 401(k) plans and a Roth IRA.

Examples from Young Money LIVE! Events

At each Young Money LIVE! event across the country, Step 4 creates significant interest and hope because the numbers don't lie. Think about it....compound interest can make a huge impact on your future financial security and even the lives of your children or future children.

I will never forget a 21 year old woman named Desiree at Hillsborough Community College in Tampa, Florida. She raised her hand after I presented to everyone the time value of money comparison during my presentation. I showed the room full of college students primarily in their 20's the difference between investing $250 per month at age 19 versus starting to invest at age 27 as we discussed before and on the chart on the previous page. To repeat, the chart simply shows that if you invested $250 per month at age 19 and then stopped investing altogether at age 27 you would have over $1.5 million at the age of 65. The chart also shows that if you waited to invest $250 per month until you were age 27 and did so every month until you were 65 you would have just over $1.2 million at the age of 65. This is nearly $300,000 less even though you invested for many more years. Desiree quickly asked "So then are you saying I should stop investing when I am 27?" I laughed because I loved her innocent question. I and several others in the class responded "absolutely not". Because if you keep investing the numbers, through compound interest, generate millions of dollars. It is so fun and such a privilege to share the Young Money Plan with young adults because they leave with a new outlook on life. Many see their dreams expanding along with their personal WHY because of these truths about money.

How Investing Affects Your Spending and Overall Financial Outlook

When you establish an automatic investing plan, it affects how you spend money. No question. It becomes easier to say "no sometimes" to things you think you need but ultimately just want. Why is this so? As you begin to see your money growing month after month, the reality of reaching some of your mid-range and long-term financial goals starts to set in. Those spending vices on Starbucks, new fashion, Chipotle, latest video games, iTunes, frozen yogurt, etc. become loosened. You now have the motivation and desire to stay within your newly created budget and financial plan. For the first time ever you are building confidence in reaching goals. And that feeling is awesome. It feels like a competition of sorts, which adds to the fun of following your personal 5 Step Money Plan, saving automatically, managing spending and now investing automatically to create long term wealth.

Young Money 5 Step Plan Action Steps

In no particular order, the following are investment services companies I highly recommend to begin Step 4 of investing automatically per month to create wealth.

Acorns (acorns.com)

Acorns is the first true micro investing company, allowing you to round up debit or credit card purchases to the nearest whole dollar and automatically invest the rest. You could easily begin investing $25 - $50 per month without much thought by simply using your debit card for purchases you already plan to make at fast food, gas stations, grocery store, iTunes, etc. Not to mention it enables you to set up automatic monthly investments in addition to your round ups.

The Acorns app and financial engine is built to help you invest commission-free into a diversified portfolio of index funds offered by the world's largest money managers: Vanguard, Blackrock, and PIMCO. You basically purchase fractional shares within the fund, automatically saving and investing small amounts of money frequently. In turn, Acorns automatically rebalances your portfolio positions for maximum performance.

Acorns basically works behind the scenes, saving and investing pennies at a time, so you don't have to. Small change may seem insignificant but history shows that even a dollar a day invested in a diversified portfolio of smaller companies over the last 50 years would be worth almost a million dollars today. Acorns is quite a game changer.

Capital One Investing (capitaloneinvesting.com)

Part of Capital One, Capital One Investing enables you to invest in stocks, mutual funds and exchange traded funds (ETF's) with no account minimums. It's easy to open an account online, receive assistance by phone and they have great mobile apps to trade and monitor your investments. Capital One Investing has an "Automatic Investment Plan" called ShareBuilder which enables you to do Step 4 very easily. You choose the dollar amount you want to invest on a monthly or bi-weekly basis and every Tuesday your money will be withdrawn from your checking account and invested in stocks, an ETF or mutual fund. Capital One Investing also has a Knowledge Center that is far from intimidating so you can understand tools, terms and investment types in no time.

Betterment (betterment.com)

Betterment is an online and fully automated investing platform that enables you to invest in stock and bond ETF's designed to provide optimal and maximum investment returns. You can create specific goals with a time horizon and Betterment will help you reach those goals by allocating your dollars, reinvesting dividends and minimizing taxes. Betterment gives you a wonderful user experience to engage with on your laptop, tablet or smartphone.

TD Ameritrade (tdameritrade.com)

I have always liked TD Ameritrade because my first brokerage account that was in my own name during college was Waterhouse Securities. Waterhouse was bought by TD Bank who then went on to buy Ameritrade. TD Ameritrade offers a very robust website to buy or trade individual stocks, mutual funds and ETF's. They have an exceptional learning and research center on their site. Unique to most big brokerages they do not have an account minimum to open up an account. There are many commission and transaction free mutual funds and ETF's to choose from.

T. Rowe Price (troweprice.com)

One of the largest mutual fund companies in the world managing over $700 billion of individual and institutional money since 1937, T. Rowe Price offers over 75 mutual funds to invest in, and has commission free representatives to help you choose which fund is right for you. Minimum investment for most of their funds is $1,000 but after that it goes down to $100 if you set up an automatic monthly investment plan. Hmm ... sound familiar? As noted in the beginning of the book, my first mutual fund at age 20 was the T. Rowe Price Science and Technology Fund.

Today, you have numerous ways to begin investing in the stock market with very little money to start and super low costs. I have shown you how wealth accumulates over time and several options of where to start investing automatically per month. Finally, a couple of additional "FYI's" when it comes to investing to increase your wealth even more.

Open a Roth IRA

To further your investment gains over the long-term, it is wise to think about having your first investment account be within a Roth IRA. A Roth IRA is an individual retirement account that offers a valuable future tax advantage. As with any investment including stocks you will pay capital gains taxes when you sell your stock, mutual fund or ETF. By setting up your mutual fund, ETF or individual stocks account within a Roth IRA you will simply pay less taxes down the road when you want to begin taking distributions.

Because you're reading this book it's very likely that you will be in a higher tax bracket when you retire than what you are in now so a Roth IRA can provide a significant tax savings for most young people. As I have discussed previously, the power of compound interest can take your monthly automatic investments to very big numbers over the next 20, 30 and 40 years. In a Roth IRA you pay no taxes on the investment income earned after you reach age 59½. This is huge. As of today, you can invest up to $5,500 per year in a Roth IRA. All of the investment companies I have listed have the Roth IRA option for you to consider.

Participate In Your 401(k) Plan or Roth 401(k) Plan

If you are currently employed by a company that offers a 401(k) retirement plan, call or run to your human resources department and ask to sign up ASAP. If not you are literally leaving free money on the table. Typically you are able to invest between 2% and 8% of your bi-weekly income in mutual funds that your employer has selected ahead of time. Your money is deducted from your paycheck *automatically*. But the big deal is that your company will likely match your investment by 25, 50 cents or even dollar for dollar. Yes, that is right. They will add to your investments if you are participating. You can't get that kind of investment return anywhere! And finally, your money is withdrawn from your paycheck *before* taxes are withdrawn, which lowers your taxable income and therefore, lowers your taxes. A 401(k) plan is a gold mine of sorts so participate if your employer has one.

Your company may also offer the option of a Roth 401(k) plan that may be equally beneficial as a traditional 401(k) plan. There are some potential long term tax benefits for going with a Roth 401(K) so simply ask questions of your HR department to make the best decision for you. Either options is a long term win.

Now that you have made a decision to invest automatically make sure you leave that money alone. Investing is for a minimum of five years. Proceeds from investments can be used to pay for a large future purchase like a down payment on a house, starting a dream business and certainly for your retirement. Unless for a true emergency, do not withdraw any returns on your investments. Instead, take advantage of the power of compound interest.

CHAPTER 5: STEP 5
Pay Yourself Second

In Step 2, I encouraged you to "pay yourself" first. And by this, I meant that before spending any of your income, you should automatically designate a portion of your paycheck to go into a savings, or a "life happens," account. The goal in paying yourself first is to begin to work towards larger financial goals. And certainly, automatic saving is an important step. It's not always easy, but it allows for financial peace and allows you to work towards the dreams and goals you identified in Step 1.

However, I want to revise this advice a bit: it is important that you actually pay yourself not first, but second. By this, I mean that it is necessary, before you think about how money can work for you that you should consider some sort of giving. Although financial success can be tremendously helpful, money and the acquisition of material goods will never provide pure happiness for anyone.

Money Cannot Create Happiness in Our Lives

On its own, money does not create the kind of peace, passion, and purpose that humans need in order to be fulfilled. That's right—money cannot give us the sense of purpose that humans need in order to be fulfilled. Instead, I believe humans need to contribute to some cause outside themselves, some greater good in order to be fulfilled and truly happy. One way to begin to do this is through charitable giving. In fact, I like to use the expression "If you are not giving, you are not living."

Not long ago at a Sunday church service in Orlando, Florida where my family was attending, a pastor discussed the importance of giving back to the community and the world that surrounds us. He used New England Patriots' star quarterback Tom Brady as an example. On the big screen he showed a clip from a *60 Minutes* interview with Brady. In the eyes of the world, Tom Brady has everything a man could desire: wealth, fame, five Super Bowl rings, a beautiful supermodel wife and adorable children. And yet, Brady says in the interview, "there's gotta be more than this." [31] Brady has what many young people might think would make them happy. And yet, when he speaks of his life, there seems to be some hollowness. He realizes that fame, money, and worldly success are not, on their own, enough to give him peace and fulfillment. Money and the acquisition of wealth and material goods are simply not enough to live a purposeful life.

Keep this quote in your mind or write it down from Corrie ten Boom: "The measure of a life is not its duration but its donation". Corrie ten Boom is best known for helping dozens of Jews escape the Nazi Holocaust and was imprisoned for it.

The Ethics of Giving Back

Religious traditions have certainly understood the importance of this principle. Take King Solomon of the Old Testament. Solomon, one of the earliest kings of the Israelites, was famous throughout his world for two things: his wisdom and his wealth. And yet, in spite of all his wealth and worldly success, Solomon realized that riches and fame were simply not enough to make a human feel fulfilled in this world. Solomon accomplished much in his life, seeing to completion his father David's great work of building a temple for the Israelites. And it is exactly this sort of project that can give people a sense of purpose.

It is believed that King Solomon wrote the Old Testament book of Proverbs, a document revered by Christians, Jews, and Muslims, and it is here that we read many of his thoughts about wealth and the acquisition of money and material goods. "Wealth is worthless in the day of wrath, but righteousness delivers from death," writes Solomon.[32] This suggests that money will ultimately not bring us happiness but that "righteousness," which is a particular way of engaging with the world and with other people, will.

We should notice, however, that Solomon is not condemning the rich for being rich. Wealth and money are not labeled as negatives by Solomon. Rather he encourages us to make positive use of wealth. Solomon also writes, "A generous man will himself be blessed, for he shares his food with the poor."[33] Clearly, wealth is a blessing and can bring fulfillment into our lives, as long as we are using our money towards making the world better.

Often, the Apostle Paul in the New Testament is misquoted as saying, "Money is the root of all evil." What Paul really writes in

1 Timothy 6:10 is that the "*love of money is the root of all evil.*"[34] In other words, pursuing money for its own sake will actually bring suffering and unhappiness into our lives. At the same time, Paul repeatedly advises taking care of those in need, notably the orphan and widow. And it is clear that this sort of caring for others requires using our money in the best way possible. Further, Paul presents this sort of giving to those in need as a positive, the opposite of stealing when he says, "Let the thief no longer steal, but rather let him labor, doing honest work with his own hands, so that he may have something to share with anyone in need."[35] It is not working and acquiring wealth that is presented as a positive good, but rather working in order to give to those who truly need it.

My Own Experiences with Money and Fulfillment

I can speak from experience when I say that pursuing money for its own sake is ultimately a hollow pursuit. I used to believe, like many Americans, that a person's financial wealth was an accurate measure of his or her success and happiness. I began investing when I was in high school, believing that if only I worked hard enough and invested smartly, I would someday be at peak happiness.

Throughout college, I worked and invested as much as I could. While some of my friends and classmates were spending their money on possessions and experiences they did not need, I took great pride in knowing that my money was working for me, by growing exponentially through wise investment. I believed that if I worked hard and deprived myself of some of the pleasures I saw my peers purchasing, I would one day be more successful and happier than anyone else. Certainly, I loved my family and friends, but I was never truly content. There was always a void in my life. I used to look around and see others who appeared to be happy and fulfilled, but I knew that I was not. I also believed that hitting a certain financial level would bring me ultimate happiness.

When I graduated college, I continued to work hard, investing as much as I could. As I did so, I looked forward to the day when I would be at peak happiness. That day always felt like it was in the future, but it was a future I could never quite achieve. At first, my goal was to have $100,000 in assets. And when that that day came and went, I did not feel happier. And so $250,000 became a mental goal, and after having reached that I still kept thinking that if only I had "enough" I'd finally be able to relax and enjoy my life. It was becoming very clear that money was taking over as number one in my life. My wife Jaci said to me one day out of the blue, "you think about money a lot." I had no clue what she was talking about because I just thought I was working hard for her and our two very young sons at the time. She was right, however. Money was on my mind 24/7.

Then, one day in my late 20's, my world came crashing down. Looking back on it, I have to say that I was basically motivated by greed, a desire to find fulfillment and a sense of worth by having more than I really needed and more than I had. This greed motivated me to make some ill-advised investments in the stock market. I chose stocks that were risky in the hope of making large amounts of money quickly. And I chose wrong. It was like gambling, putting money in the wrong places in the hope of making a lot of money, money that in retrospect I didn't even need. The result was losing nearly 40% of my net worth over a two year period. That's right; I lost nearly half of my assets by making poor investment choices based on greed. Nothing else. I was devastated.

Because my only measure of success and self-worth, at the time, was how much money I had, losing this much was a tremendous blow to my sense of self. I felt like a complete failure. In many ways, it was this experience that caused me to question my purpose in life and my own worth as a human being. However, I can see now that I needed this sort of humbling. It caused me to reassess my values and what I wanted from life. Once I got over the initial shock of losing so much and the attendant blow to my ego, I realized that I was not significantly less happy with less money. I realized that, like so many before me, the pursuit of money for its own sake is ultimately empty. Having more had not made me significantly happier. I was forced to admit that there had to be more to life than just the pursuit of wealth.

As I worked to bounce back from this tremendous financial loss, I reexamined my motives in pursuing wealth. I knew that I had a good mind for finance and that with work and wise investments, I would someday recover what I had lost. But I also knew from experience that this alone would not make me happy. I came to understand that my worth as a person could not be measured in dollars and cents, nor was peace and fulfillment correlated to how much was in my bank account.

The Story of Mia

Over the last several years I have shared the story of a young girl named Mia during our Young Money LIVE! speaking tour across the country. It's part of my life story and part of my Step 5 of the Young Money Plan. So, who is Mia? Well, it all started on my fifth date with Jaci, who was my girlfriend at the time and my wife today. We were having dinner at a quaint restaurant in Mount Adams, which overlooks downtown Cincinnati and the Ohio River. During our date, Jaci began sharing some of her dreams in life which I thought was fun and vulnerable at the same time. She said things like "I want to stay at that hotel on the water in Tahiti someday" I agreed that would be a lot of fun. I opened up a little bit with her and shared some of my dreams including wanting to learn how to play the piano. My dreams were not as deep as hers especially when she shared one final dream over desert. She said "I would really like to adopt a little girl from China someday." I remember the moment vividly. All the fun we were having seemed to subside in that instant. Wow, that was some dream I thought. I did not know anyone who adopted and was really clueless about adoption. I also thought it would take a ton of money to adopt. Later on that evening after taking her home to her apartment I sat on my bed in my apartment and thought about how much I really liked Jaci. So much that for the first time in my life the thought of marriage came to mind. But then I thought "If we get married are we really going to adopt a little girl from China?" I certainly hoped not.

Eighteen months later, Jaci and I were married. Jaci was pregnant with our first son Jack several months later. For 10 consecutive years, she would bring up adopting a girl from

China. She never coerced me to adopt or applied any type of pressure. I was just focused on my life, our current family and never said yes or no. I really never said anything in hopes that her desire to adopt would somehow go away.

After going through my personal financial hardship due to the foolish decisions I made a couple of years before I finally realized that I was getting in the way of my wife's desire and dream to adopt a little girl from China. And I was beginning to realize that my life was not all about me and my happiness. We made the decision to adopt Mia Elizabeth Qingfang Romer in 2005, and went to China to bring her home in 2007. Qingfang was the name the orphanage gave her after she was literally dropped off on the steps as a baby.

Mia has been a tremendous blessing in our lives and in my life particularly. I share her story of adoption because most people feel it is a form of giving. Actually, I have been the one that has been given to. Funny how giving plays itself out. Mia is now 13 years old and she makes an impression on me nearly every day. Step 5 of the Young Money Plan is all about giving. It should be a part of everyone's personal financial plan so you can truly live life with a greater purpose.

Remember, there is nothing wrong with having a large number of assets, a lot of money, driving a nice car, or owning a vacation home or two. However, simply owning these things or having a fat bank or investment account will not bring you happiness. I learned over time, however, that using money to positively affect people and good in the world can give one a sense of purpose, peace and joy. I continue to feel more purpose each and every day and you can too.

Your Money at Work for Others

Once a month, five women, all mothers, gather around a table inside the Gator Grill in New Castle Virginia. Over pancakes, eggs and mugs of steaming coffee they talk about how to make their 'Field of Dreams,' a planned baseball complex for the community, come true. Their goal is four baseball diamonds complete with dugouts and bleachers, a central two-story media complex that will house announcers for each game, a concession stand, bathrooms and storage for equipment for maintaining the fields.

They currently have one field constructed. From the home plate and bleachers, players and fans can see the majestic skyline of the Blue Ridge Mountains and a small river that runs along the edge of the property. If anything, the view itself keeps their dream alive.

These are not ordinary women. They are mothers, but they're also bankers, teachers, and University faculty and business owners. They have a vision, a plan and a 501(c) (3) non-profit designation. In a town where the average wages are between $18,000 and $35,000, a $2 million dollar baseball complex could seem like an impossible goal. But it's not. Why, because people in New Castle give whether they can 'afford to' or not.

A pavilion is planned for an open space next to, and overlooking the river. The concrete foundation for the pavilion, along with the benches and building, and the small footbridge to cross a meandering stream, are a donation. A father whose daughter was killed along with two other teenagers in a pre-graduation automobile accident is donating the materials and labor. He's building the pavilion so his other daughter can be married there in the spring, and to honor the family's loss of their child.

The baseball complex, when complete, will allow the town to host baseball and softball tournaments. Renting the fields and facilities to other conferences and tournaments will bring in much needed money to the town and help finance the daycare center where over half of the town's population leaves their children each day as they go to work outside the community.

The day care center recently lost government funding of more than $65,000 and must make up the difference, or shut down the school. Most families could barely afford the lower than average daycare rates. Raising the rates isn't an option.

New Castle is a working class town. People commute to nearby Roanoke, or Salem, 25 miles away. Losing their only day care provider would be devastating. People would have to move, give up jobs, and potentially suffer even greater hardship if they can't find affordable day care. But it's about more than money. Parents told the Craig County Board of Supervisors they know and trust the staff at the childcare center, which is the size of a small elementary school. Many of the parents attended the center as children and are now sending their own children to the school.

Building the baseball complex, making enough money to support the childcare center and providing tourism dollars is about the town surviving as a town too, one parent told the board. When families start leaving, jobs disappear, businesses close down and soon New Castle will be a ghost town. It's not there yet, but the women keep the fear at bay by buttering biscuits, talking about fundraisers and looking for donations.

While the town of New Castle itself isn't a charity, they do have citizens who have formed this nonprofit to raise money to build the baseball complex, a complex they have officially dubbed "The Field of Dreams."

This is what charity is all about—real people with real lives. I didn't want to open this chapter with a lot of facts about charity for the same reason I don't adhere to the conventional money management rules. I'm talking about the rules that focus on fear and advise putting part of your paycheck into savings or investment before paying your bills and spending money on other things. I say, what's more important than paying yourself first is first giving back to create a better life for others now or in the future

When you give, you shouldn't just be writing a check to make tax season a little better. Giving is not about numbers, about seeing how much money you can give, or how little you can give and still feel good. Giving is about changing lives. Giving is about finding charities like the Craig County Recreational Center, and making a difference in the lives of the children and the children to follow.

The parents in New Castle understand this. Volunteers mow, drag, chalk the base lines and maintain that one baseball diamond every week. No one gets paid. The community wants their 'Field of Dreams' and they're making it happen, one field at a time. One local business built the dugouts and benches. Another donated equipment. Two local stonemasons took rock donated by another citizen and used the stones to build a 20-foot sign announcing the 'Field of Dreams' and the 'Craig County Recreational Center. Other parents and volunteers simply show up to do whatever it takes to make the field playable.

Charity and giving is about more than money. It's an attitude. It's part of your character and should be part of your business. How you give and where you give is about more than picking a safe organization. It's about reaching out and finding an organization where your donation improves lives.

Giving is in Our DNA

Giving is not only traditional; it's in our DNA. As human beings, we feel almost compelled to help others when we can afford to, and sometimes even when we can't.

According to Giving USA, 2015 was a record year for charitable giving. Donations from America's individuals, estates, foundations and corporations totaled nearly $373 billion!. That doesn't include the billions hours of volunteer time. I doubt the thousands of hours New Castle residents spent building their Field of Dreams is on any official list, and that's not the point. For every 10 hours noted in some database somewhere (my wild guess), there are hundreds, maybe thousands of hours that go undocumented, but certainly not unnoticed.

The Corporation for National & Community Service reports that 64.3 percent of Americans volunteer every year in some form of formal organization. That doesn't include people who volunteer for local causes, or who simply help neighbors, donate to various causes or participate informally in their neighborhoods and communities. Over 60,000 new charities are created each year. As of 2013, there were over 1.6 million nonprofit organizations. Even in tough economic times, Americans are generous with their time, resources and money. Natural disasters always bring out extra generosity.

When Hurricane Katrina hit the U.S. Gulf Coast in 2005, people stepped up to give the largest outpouring of charitable support in the history of the United States – giving approximately $5.3 billion – in one year, for victims of an environmental disaster.

Paul Newman's Foundation has donated $300 Million of profits to his Hole in the Wall camps for kids with serious diseases, and helping the nonprofit charity, Feeding America.

While conventional wisdom says the rich stay rich by holding onto their money, that's just not true. In 2006, oil tycoon T. Boone Pickens made a $20 million gift to Oklahoma State University. He had only one stipulation for his gift. He insisted that the university find 25 additional alumni ages 65 to 85. Those alum had to agree to have the institution take out a $10-million life-insurance policy for them, naming the university as beneficiary. The university actually found 27 such participants. The first insurance policies for the alum went into effect in February 2007.

That same year, President George W. Bush enacted the Pension Protection Act. The Act includes a number of charitable giving incentives and reforms. It defines and regulates donor advised funds. The Act allows donors, for only two years, to make contributions up to $100,000 per year from their individual retirement account (IRA) to a qualifying charity. It does more to ensure that gift giving is real, and not simply abused for tax purposes. The Act also eliminates fractional gifts of art; disallows charitable deductions for taxpayers who do not itemize; redefine gifts of clothing and household items to prevent abuse; increases penalty excise taxes, and promulgates new regulatory requirements for Type III supporting organizations.

In 2006, Warren Buffett announced a gift of $43.5 billion in Berkshire Hathaway stock to a number of private foundations and charities. Most surprisingly, the largest disbursement would be to the Bill & Melinda Gates Foundation ($31 billion), making it the largest single charitable gift in history.

There are literally millions of charitable donations of all sizes, from handfuls of loose change to millions of dollars, happening every day. The most current charitable trend is the 'Giving Pledge,' which invites the wealthiest individuals and families in America to commit to giving the majority of their wealth to charitable causes of all kinds.

Every year, Forbes Magazine lists the names of the top 50 charities in America. Giving is big business. If you're not a part of it, you're missing out professionally as well as personally. It's a well-known fact that a lot of business is conducted outside the office, either at dinners or conferences or on the golf course. But business is done at charity events as well. It's not only a great place to network, but to find other vendors, businesses and corporations who support the same causes you do.

More Than a Feeling

While those who give regularly report "feeling good," as a primary motivator for their giving, there's more than just "a good feeling" involved.

Medical science tells us that feeling good is ultimately reflected in our biology or health. In a 2006 study at the National Institute of Health, Jorge Moll and his colleagues found that when people give to charities, it activates regions of the brain associated with pleasure, social connection, and trust, creating a "warm glow" effect. Giving is also linked to the release of oxytocin, a hormone released when babies are born, when mothers breastfeed and when people have sex, cuddle, kiss or even hug for several minutes or longer. It's the hormone that creates the "helper's high," and can last for up to two hours. This helper's high and the associated hormones have been found to lead to better health in the giver.

On average, elderly people who volunteer for 2 or more organizations were 44 percent less likely to die over a 5-year period than non-volunteers, even after factoring in things like age, exercise habits, and even negative habits like smoking. Stephanie Brown of the University of Michigan led a study about charity, finding that individuals who provided practical help to friends, family, neighbors or relatives, or gave emotional support to their spouses, had a lower risk of dying over a five-year period than those who didn't. Those who received the help weren't linked to a reduced risk.

In her book, *The How of Happiness*, Sonja Lyubomirsky writes "Being kind and generous leads you to perceive others more positively and more charitably, which fosters a heightened sense of interdependence and cooperation in your social community."

The gratitude elicited from our generosity builds social and personal bonds and boosts individual happiness in the giver and the recipient. Generosity is contagious. When we give we create a ripple effect that spreads through our family, our neighborhood and our community. Studies show that when one person acts with generosity that observers are most likely to do the same, spreading generosity through as much as three degrees of separation.

Ask the police chief in New Castle if a baseball complex will affect him, and he'll say "Yes!" Not only does participating in a sport create a positive outlet for kids in small towns, a place to go, goals and sports keep crime rates, drinking and teenage sex rates down. Parents and citizens who come together to volunteer also tend to strengthen community bonds, network and support each other's businesses.

So now that you know giving has health benefits as well as social, business and even tax related benefits, let's talk about where and how you can make long and short-term gifts that make a difference.

Determining How Often and How Much to Give

Many organizations and businesses elect to donate monthly, with a bonus donation at Christmas or at the end of each financial quarter. Others choose to make a lump sum donation at the beginning or end of each year. Some organizations have 'wish lists' of machinery, appliances, supplies, and items they need year round. Ask if a charity you're considering has such a list. Donate when, and as you're able to meet specific needs.

How you give depends on your situation. If you do decide to give once or twice a year, set aside the funds each week or month to ensure the money is there when it comes time to write the check or transfer through the charity's secure online donation platform.

There is no right or wrong amount to give. Organizations appreciate every donation they get. Don't worry about competing with other businesses or individuals over donation amounts either. It's not a competition. Give as you feel you can give. If money isn't an option, consider giving 'in-kind' donations of time, resources, materials or equipment loans. I love this Bible passage about giving in 2 Corinthians 9:7. It pretty much sums it up. "Each man should give what he has decided in his heart to give, not reluctantly or under compulsion, for God loves a cheerful giver."

Give Time

Volunteer for any organization you're thinking of donating money to. This gives you a chance to see how well, or poorly, the organization is managed and how well they meet their mission goals.

Give to People and Organizations You Know

Giving is good no matter where you give to make a difference. There's just something even more special about giving to someone in your local community, or to a cause or organization that you know and that you can see the results of your donation. Being able to fund a scholarship that sends a child to summer camp, or buys them a scouting uniform or sports equipment can be as big a thrill to you as it is to them.

Local churches and synagogues always welcome donations of food, time and services. Schools always need supplies, lunch funds for those children whose parents can't afford hot lunches, and even canned food to send home with certain children in what many schools call their "backpack feeding program." They give children backpacks filled with food each Friday so the children have something to eat over the weekends.

There are hundreds of opportunities to make an impact in your community. Look for them. If you don't want to give locally, give to national organizations that have a local impact—like Meals On Wheels. Give first. Give joyfully. Change someone's life.

CHAPTER 6: THE OTHER MONEY STUFF
(Credit, Debt and Taxes)

The 5 Step Plan outlined in the first five chapters of this book can absolutely allow you to create a life that fits your dreams. Yet, there are other personal finance topics that you need to know about so you have a broad understanding of how money works when it comes to things like credit, debt and taxes. In Chapter 7 I will cover big ticket purchase decisions like buying a house, a car and what required insurance you need to have to protect the wealth that you will build for yourself over time.

Many young people think that poor credit only affects things like vehicle purchases. Wrong. Your financial health can determine what kinds of jobs you can get, what kind of apartment you can be approved for, and whether or not you can get the kind of credit rating you need to keep your expenses low for the long term. Did you know the price of your car insurance is linked not just to your age and number of accidents or tickets you've had, but to your credit score as well? A poor credit score is a red flag, telling companies that you're not responsible and can't be trusted to pay your bills or be a good driver. I know that's not always the case, but that's how companies think.

Choices in life become much more limited when you continue to battle poor financial health. Poor financial health includes high credit card debt, a low credit score, unbalanced checking accounts, no investments, no savings, no emergency fund and spending more than you're making every month.

Good financial health means a good credit score, no more than a 30 percent utilization of your total allotted credit, a savings account with two to three months of living expenses (rent, utilities, etc.) socked away for emergencies and investments in a mix of stocks and bonds. If you need to buy a car, you have the down payment of at least 25%. If you want to take a vacation, fly to a job interview, volunteer to help build a school in Africa, you have the money. While money can't buy happiness, it can buy choices. And it's choices, coupled with life purpose, that make us happy, fulfilled and productive.

The best paying jobs are often linked to financial responsibility—banking, investments, accounting, management and more. Poor credit scores can knock you out of the running for good-paying jobs in many industries, including emergency services, law enforcement, medical and financial fields.

You may be able to afford a nice apartment, but a poor credit score is one of the primary reasons most young (and older) people are denied on housing applications. Even if you can show proof of income, with a poor credit score you'll most likely have to provide a large deposit and/or have a cosigner.

If you're out of school and have a job, you may need to buy a car to get to and from work. A poor credit score may not keep you from buying a car, but it can result in finance rates of up to 18 percent or more versus 0 to 5 percent auto finance rates. See where this is going? Poor financial health affects all aspects of your life whether you know it or not. Take heart. You're not alone in your struggle with debt and credit.

According to the Consumer Protection Financial Bureau, student loan debt has passed the $1 trillion dollar mark. In 2010, the average student graduated from college with $25,000 in loan debt, plus an average of $3,173 on their credit cards.[36] Unless you have parents who planned for your college well, or you have a full-ride scholarship, chances are your postgraduate plans will include a hefty loan payment each month.

Okay, it's true, not everyone goes to a four college or university. In fact, half of those aged 18-to-21 years of age don't go to college. However, many of them do attend trade schools or two year community colleges. And their student loans also pile up. They're often unable to finish school or become employed even with training in a trade.[37]

In many cultures, people in the 18-to-25-year old age group are considered adults. They either go to college or are employed and working towards buying a home, getting married and raising children. In the United States, however, this age group is considered "transitioning adults." They are considered to be more likely to demonstrate risk taking behaviors, and to engage in poor financial decision making, leading to more stress and greater health risks.[38]

There have been hundreds of studies done on young people and debt and the consensus is that debt is directly related to a lack of financial knowledge, or "financial illiteracy"."[39] Financial literacy, or the ability to use knowledge and skills to manage one's financial resources and income effectively, determines what kind of life you'll have. Since your ability and skill levels will be used to plan your retirement, stock market participation, portfolio choices and even your health plans, it's critical to understand how to manage your money. Learning to manage money is one of the primary steps from transitioning from childhood to adulthood. The habits you create now will stay with throughout your life.

Yes, lots of people have debt and get by, but at what cost? You can't make debt, taxes or bad financial decisions go away by simply ignoring them. Instead of dreading the idea of understanding and managing your money, think of it as a job skill, game or competition. Once you get a handle on how to budget, save, spend, invest and give, money management will become second nature, just like driving a car or riding a bike. You'll know what to do without having to think about every little move you make. Just as there are hazards on the road that you need to look out for, there are hazards in your financial path too. Let's first break it down and look at the pitfalls and traps you can get into with credit cards and credit card debt.

Credit Cards

It used to be the day you registered for college classes; you were offered the opportunity to get a credit card, no strings or requirements or credit proof attached. The Card Act of 2009 changed all that. It made it a little harder to get a credit card. The law now requires people under the age of 21 to declare on the credit card application that they have sufficient income/ assets to cover the new card's monthly payments (usually 3 percent of the limit) or have a cosigner (mom or dad) in order to qualify. Still, it's not as hard as it should be to get a card.

If you've never handled or had access to large sums of money, $1,000 to $2,500 credit limit on a new credit card can be pretty tempting stuff. Like most students with a new card, it can be tempting to run right out and use the card on some new jeans, shoes or electronics that otherwise you cannot afford, telling yourself you will pay off the card soon.

There are thousands of overspending stories I have heard from young millennials from nearly all fifty states after they received their first credit card. Many felt they would be responsible only to find themselves swiping with the card out of convenience and seeing their balance rise with not enough income to pay it back. Months and years go by with a high credit card balance and a heaviness that comes with drowning in consumer credit card debt. Not to mention paying late on the card once or twice a year that causes a negative effect on your credit score. Thus, the cycle of living paycheck to paycheck can start and last decades for many.

But I know that is not the kind of life you want for yourself. You have begun to dream about your life and what you want it to look like. It all starts with how you manage your current income, no matter how small. Like I have said many times on stage, "if you can't manage your poor college student income now how do you expect to manage your hopeful out of college income later".

Most people don't realize credit cards haven't always been around. Our country was founded on a cash basis, not on getting credit. Even now many people are moving away from credit and going to a cash only plan, buying only the items they can afford to pay cash for when they buy. There are several reasons for having credit cards, but ultimately it's up to you to decide what's best for your situation. If you decide to get a credit card, there are several things you should know before you apply for one.

OPENING A NEW CREDIT CARD CAN TEMPORARILY DROP YOUR CREDIT SCORE.
Before you open a new credit card, be aware that a new card can drop your credit score by up to 15 percent. Why? Because part of the formula for calculating your credit is based upon what's called your "credit age." There's the age of your oldest credit card or loan account and the age of your newest account. Opening a new card can lower the averages of those accounts. However, your *credit utilization rate* will be lowered which positively affects your credit score.

Your credit utilization rate comprises 30 percent of your total credit score. A credit utilization rate is the ratio of your credit card balances to your credit card limits as listed on your credit report. For instance, if you have a credit card limit of $1,000 and your credit card balance (what you owe) is $300, then your credit utilization is 30 percent, right where it should be. Even if you're paying off your bills in full every month, using more than the 30 percent of credit you're allotted can lower your score. The lower your credit utilization the better, because it shows you're only using a small amount of the credit that you've been given. To find out what your current credit utilization is, find your total credit limit on all your accounts. Divide your credit card balances (what you owe), by your credit limit then multiply by 100.

DOES THE CREDIT CARD COMPANY REPORT TO ALL THREE CREDIT BUREAUS?
Credit cards are good for one thing—building your credit. Nearly all credit card issuers and lenders have to report your payment

history to the credit bureaus which start to assign a score for you based on your timely repayments. There are three primary credit bureaus: Transunion, Equifax and Experian. Their independent scores may be averaged together for a credit score. Some lenders may only look at one or two of the scores when deciding to lend you money or extend you credit. Some companies only report to one bureau when reporting your score. Companies that report to the credit bureau include the bank or credit union that holds your home mortgage or car loan, your credit card issuer and the bank or credit union that holds any personal loans. If you're behind on payments to your utility or cell phone provider they won't immediately report you to a credit bureau. However, they could hand over your account to a debt collector which, in time, could be reported to one of the bureaus.

What is the interest rate?

Typically, the better your credit, the lower the interest rate for your credit card. Rates can still vary from 5 to 25 percent so make sure you know what you're paying for the convenience of having a credit card. Your goal should be to pay off your credit card in full every month and not incur interest charges in the first place so it really should not matter to you what the interest rate is.

What are the fees involved?

ANNUAL FEE. Some credit card companies charge an annual fee of $49 - $199 for the frequent flyer points or other perks they offer you when using the card. Many cards do not charge an annual fee. An annual fee is typically applied to your first bill.

CASH ADVANCE FEE. This fee is charged to you if you use your credit card like an ATM card. There is a limit to how much cash you can take out against your card. Highly recommend to not to use this feature of your credit card because your credit card is not a bank account. It's simply a short term loan that needs to be paid back.

LATE FEE. Late fees can cost you as much as $39 and can trigger an automatic interest rate increase of up to 30 percent! Many card companies offer low interest rate teasers to get you to sign up, then raise the interest rate or have other hidden fees that can really hurt you financially if you're not aware of them. Look for the term APR (Average Percentage Rate) in the fine print.

OTHER FEES. Most credit cards have foreign transaction fees so if you travel a lot you may want to take that into consideration before you charge away.

Credit Bureaus

WHAT IS A CREDIT BUREAU AND WHY DO THEY HAVE SO MUCH POWER OVER MY LIFE? Credit bureaus are an organization that collects information about your spending and payment history. The information they collect is a strong indicator of your spending habits. By tracking your previous loan performance and payment records a credit bureau is able to predict your future behavior when it comes to borrowing and repaying a loan. If you're consistently late paying your bills now, chances are very good you'll be consistently late paying them in the future, making you a credit risk. Credit bureaus tell lenders what their risk is if they make a loan to you. That credit risk number is called your credit score. A very poor to below average score is 300 – 599. An average score is 600 to 699 and a good score is 700 to 800. Anything between 800 -850 is deemed excellent.

WHAT IS DEBT? Debt is the obligation you owe a lender or merchant. If you charge a $100 item on your credit card at a store in the mall your debt is $100. It may increase to more than $100, due to interest charges, if you do not pay off the purchase by the card due date (around 25 days).

There is good debt and bad debt. Good debt typically covers three areas: education, housing and transportation. But let's briefly discuss each so you are clear on what I am saying. Education debt refers to student loans to cover tuition and book fees while attending college. Studies have shown for decades that someone with a college degree will earn more than someone who only has a high school degree. So taking on some education debt is good debt due to the future earnings that come from your college degree. Buying a home by taking on mortgage debt is considered good debt. As long as you are able to put a solid down payment (ie....20% of the loan) and weigh your monthly payment against your monthly income so you don't become "house poor". There are tax advantages for being a home owner and over time real estate prices have risen as well. So housing debt is good debt if managed well from the beginning. The final "good debt" scenario may take the form of a car loan. If you have just been hired by a company that has positive upside for you and your family but you have no transportation then taking on car loan debt is not a bad thing. Choosing an affordable car (new or used) is the key to not making your car loan debt a bad financial decision.

Bad debt is any debt you take on for things you want, but simply can't afford. Paying for a week in Florida on spring break on your credit card is simply not good debt if you don't have the money to pay it off within the 25 day grace period. In fact, the worst kind of debt is credit-card card debt since it usually carries the highest interest rates.

Taxes

Understanding taxes is important to your long term financial health. Taxes are what you pay on your income, your assets, investments and property. If you're working for an employer they take out taxes to cover things like FICA, Social Security and Medicare taxes. If you don't pay your taxes, or you pay them late, you can not only incur *more* debt, the government can seize your assets (car, home, etc.), bank accounts, investments and whatever financial resources you have in order to pay off that debt. You can also be fined additional costs, and in extreme cases, do jail time. If you're investing, saving and earning money you want to ensure you know what you owe the state and federal government in annual or quarterly taxes, and then pay it on time. If you don't feel comfortable figuring out what you owe and when, then make a strong effort to learn, and consult a tax expert while you do.

Payroll tax deductions include the following:

- Federal income tax withholding
- Social Security tax withholding
- Medicare tax withholding
- State income tax withholding (if your state has a state income tax)
- Various local tax withholdings (such as city, county, or school district taxes, state disability or unemployment insurance).

If you're employed, your employer will figure and pay those taxes. If you're working for yourself, you're expected to estimate your earnings and pay your own taxes since you're the 'employer.'

Don't Panic

I know this seems like a lot of information to take in all at once. The good news is you don't have to do it all at once! Let's go back to the healthy body metaphor. You don't walk into a gym all out of shape and expect to get that hard, buff, sexy, fit body in a day, or a week or even a few months. You start out with small weights, and 15 minutes of cardio. You increase your workout and weights as your body begins to respond to your routine. It's the same way with your financial health. Begin with what you understand and apply it. As you become more confident and financially healthy, you up your routine. As you're saving money, start reading about investing. After you've saved some money (as I did with my lawn care business as a teenager), invest some of that money. The stronger and healthier you get financially, by budgeting, saving, and investing, the more financial challenges you can take on. You can learn about taxes, real estate, and other financial tools that may intimidate you over time.

If you've ever walked into a gym and seen body builders lifting their weight in iron, or watched people on the treadmill run for hours at a time while you struggled to walk for 20 minutes, you have seen what it takes to get healthy. You may have thought, "I'll never be that strong," but if you keep working out, a year later you'll laugh at your fears because your body has responded to the challenge. Now you're one of the people who make 30-45 minutes on the treadmill look effortless.

If you're a college student you know that when you walk into any class for the first time there's a lot you don't know. It takes weeks and hours of lectures, reading and studying, taking, failing, and passing tests to successfully complete the course.

You don't always get an 'A' on every test. The tests you do well on are a result of study, application and understanding. Financial expertise comes the same way. You focus, study, apply the principles you learn, and then fail or succeed. If you succeed, you build on that success. If you fail, go back and study and try again until you do succeed. Some skills are easier to learn and apply than others. Some skills take days; others take months to master.

You Can Do It

I guarantee the effort you put in to follow this 5 Step Plan to financial success will be worth it. You have learned about the wise use of credit, good and bad debt and the role of taxes in your financial life in this chapter.

Because money can be such an emotional issue, and is usually tied to our early experiences and influences in life, learning to manage your money can involve looking at a lot of other factors as well. Your relationship to money is often tied to how your parents handled money. We learn what we're exposed to. If your parents weren't good with money, chances are you won't be either. But that doesn't mean you can't learn to be good, or learn to be better. You can. If you're still feeling overwhelmed, scared or uncertain about money, don't worry. You're not alone.

- Studies and statistics show that 86% of students would rather learn about money now before making real world mistakes.[40]
- The majority (52%) of young adults between the ages of 23 and 28 consider "making better choices about managing money" the single most important issue for individual Americans to act on today.[41]
- 64% say financial fitness is more important than physical fitness, and the majority (51%) believe that financial education in school, grades K-12, is more important than both physical education (31%) and sex education (18%) combined.[42]
- Three out of four admit to having made mistakes with their money when they arrived on their college campus.[43]

Remember, you don't become a financial powerhouse all at once. You begin one step at a time.

CHAPTER 7: MORE MONEY STUFF
(Buying a Car, Insurance and Housing)

This chapter rounds out the other personal finance stuff that you need to know so you have less money stress in the short and long term. In this chapter, the focus will be on the larger purchases you will make in the near future like buying a car and a house. We will also focus on why it is super important to protect your growing wealth through insurance.

Major purchases should fit in your current budget and your long-term goals. Before you decide to make a purchase, you should always review your personal budget to make sure that you have the discretionary income to take on a new monthly payment or the cash to buy the item outright. You should be able to live within your income even after you make the purchase. No purchase is ever worth putting yourself in financial stress.

Buying a Car

If you have ever gone through the car buying process, you know that it is not as easy as just pulling up to the auto dealership and making the purchase. If you want to find the best deal for your money, you need to put some work in!

For most people buying a car will be the second largest purchase of their life aside from buying a house. There are many options available when it comes to selecting and buying a car. Let's explore the options you have for selecting the right car and your options for where to buy the car.

In the past, the only way to look for and buy a car was to visit a dealership. Of course, with technology and the Internet, there are many options when it comes to shopping for a vehicle. Consumers are now able to browse various websites, such as cars.com, truecar.com, carsforsale.com, and many other sites in order to find the right vehicle. Before a consumer even visits the dealership, he or she can find out the price of the vehicle, the features, condition and view pictures of the vehicle. This eliminates the unnecessary time spent driving from one dealership to another. These Internet sites also provide the means for comparison shopping. You can find the best deals without even leaving the comforts of your home.

There are those that still like to visit the dealerships, and that certainly is another option when it comes to selecting the right vehicle. Test driving the vehicle is important. You want to make sure that the style, size, and drive of the vehicle will fit your needs and wants.

Once you have selected the vehicle that you want to purchase, you have several options of where to buy the vehicle and from whom. The websites previously mentioned will have vehicles that are for sale in all 50 states. If you are willing to drive a certain distance, it is possible to find a better deal than from a local car dealer. More consumers are driving longer distances in order to save money on their purchase due to the internet's ability to comparison shop.

Many car dealerships also have their own business websites. If you find a vehicle on one of these sites, many times you can begin the application process before you even arrive at the dealership. This will save you time and also let you know if you would be approved or not for the vehicle. If buying from a dealership is not something you enjoy, another option is buying directly from another consumer.

Websites, such as Craigslist and eBay offer consumers the option of purchasing a vehicle directly from an individual. With this process, you would eliminate the need of going through a dealership and you can usually find a good deal. As with all purchases, it is important to conduct research on the vehicle before making the decision. You should consider the safety of the car, any warranties that might be available, the price, and also what amount you might be offered for a trade-in (if that applies to your situation).

Anytime you purchase a vehicle, especially a pre-owned vehicle, there is a certain amount of risk. By doing additional research and using the tools that are available to you, you can make a more informed decision about the vehicle that will best suit your needs and wants. The selection and purchasing of a vehicle does not have to be a stressful and time consuming process. You have more control over this process than ever before. Make sure to ask about any warranties that might be available. Usually with pre-owned cars from individuals, the car is sold as-is, so you are taking a risk.

College Graduate Program Incentives

If you are in college or recently graduated, many manufactures like Toyota, Honda, General Motors, Ford, Hyundai, Kia and others offer additional new car incentives within their college graduate programs. Some car companies offer $400 - $1,000 off a new vehicle upon showing proof you are a student or have recently graduated from a four year, two year, community college or trade school. Most offer this discount on top of other dealer discounts and incentives so be sure to ask questions.

Financing Your Car

Now that you have found the car of your dreams or one that fits your budget, you need to consider how you will pay for the vehicle. If you purchase a new vehicle, you likely will have the option to buy or lease. There are pros and cons to both of these purchasing options. When you buy a vehicle, you take out a loan and repay the money over a certain time period; three to five years is common for car loans. Once the vehicle is paid off, you own the vehicle outright and it is all yours.

When you lease a vehicle, there is no loan involved and you pay the leasing company a monthly fee for having the vehicle. When the lease term is up (usually two to three years), you have two options: buy the vehicle for the remainder of the value of the car (this is the residual value) or give the car back and start the car buying process all over. If you are someone who likes to change cars every few years, this can be a good option. It is important to make sure you don't go over the mileage given to you (usually 36,000 miles for a three year lease) or you will pay a hefty penalty at the end. Also, if you don't want to have a car payment all the time, leasing may not be the best option. It is important to weigh all of your options and carefully consider what will be best for you in the long-term.

Depending on where you decide to purchase the car from, financing might be available from the seller. Most car dealerships have on-site financing available because they work with several bank lenders that approve loans for their customers. If you choose this route, make sure you are told the terms of the loan, such as the interest rate, repayment term, and any other fees that might be added on. The interest rates can be higher for the vehicle, so consider shopping around if the rate is too high for you. Of course, you can also go to your own bank or credit union and apply for the loan. If this is your first loan, you might need a co-signer, such as a parent or other relative but I frown on nearly all co-signed loans.

Whether you buy or lease, you might be asked for a down payment. This is especially true for new cars. Consider how much cash you want to invest in the car and how much liquid cash you have available. The more you put down, the lower your monthly payment will be when you purchase the vehicle. The down payment will usually not impact your monthly lease payment.

Purchasing a car is a major decision and should be taken seriously. Doing your homework and finding the best car for your budget and situation will help you to stay financially healthy and be able to enjoy the new car for years to come.

What About Buying a Used Car?

I have bought new and used cars over the years. There are advantages and disadvantages to each. If you are buying some wheels for the first time you need to know these differences.

Advantages of Buying a Used Car

- Depending on how old the car is the purchase price will be much less than a new car.
- The rate of depreciation over time will typically be less than a new vehicle.

Disadvantages of Buying a Used Car

- Depending on the car's mileage you will likely incur more costs for repairs and maintenance than a new car that has a comprehensive warranty for the first 3 years or 36,000 miles. Some new cars have a manufacturer's warranty that covers 10 years or 100,000 miles.
- Depending on the car's age there may not be the same safety features as a new car provides today.

I have experienced used cars that did not require much repair and maintenance and drove it for many years. I have also experienced used cars that were very frustrating because of the constant and expensive repairs. There really is no right or wrong answer to buying new vs. used. My recommendation if you are buying new is that you hold on to the car for at least seven or more years so you can benefit financially. The quality in most new cars is superior compared to ten years ago. Set a savings goal to put at least a 20% down payment on the new car, which will lower your monthly payment. Ultimately, you will want to set a mid-range goal to pay off your car before the end of the loan term. This will save you dollars in interest by paying off the loan early.

Buying a House

Home sweet home! The biggest purchase you will likely ever make is the purchase of a home. Your home usually makes up 30% or more of your monthly income, so this is not a purchase to take lightly! Before you start looking for your dream home, you should first consider how much you can actually afford. This will help you to narrow down your search and not give you false hope about what type of house you can afford.

Nearly all people require financing to purchase a home, so your ability to access financing or get approved for a loan will likely determine the price range of the home you can buy. You should also consider your future financial situation as well. Mortgages are usually in place for 15 to 30 years, so many factors in your life can change during that time.

Most lenders will look at your income, current debts, and your credit history in order to assess your ability to assume and payback a mortgage. Your credit score is also an important tool that lenders consider. Lenders will also request verification of employment and income. Be prepared to share a lot of financial information with the lender. The house buying process can be grueling, so preparing can make the process easier.

As was stated above, most lenders do their own calculations of how much debt you can take on based on your monthly gross income. Most lenders agree that no more than 33 percent of your gross monthly income should go towards your monthly housing cost. This also includes the monthly insurance and real estate taxes that you will owe on the property. Consider your current monthly income. What is 33% of your monthly income? Understanding this number will give you a rough estimate of how much you might be approved for by the lender.

Before you even start looking for a home, it is a good idea to talk to a lender to see how much you can afford and also to get pre-approved. A pre-approval is based on the initial information that you have provided to the lender. Having a pre-approval will show any potential seller that you are a serious buyer and your offers are more likely to be considered strongly.

Another area to consider when deciding to buy a home is the down payment. Mortgages require a **down payment**, or a percentage of the purchase price paid in cash upon purchase. Most buyers use cash from savings and investments, the proceeds of a house they are selling or a family gift.

The size of the down payment does not affect the price of the house, but it can affect the cost of the financing. For a certain house price, the larger the down payment, the smaller the mortgage and, all things being equal, the lower the monthly payments. Assuming you are a first-time homebuyer, there may be special programs to assist you with financing your new home. Check with your lender for more details.

Searching for the House

Now that you know how much house you can afford, you can begin the home search. Typically, buyers use a realtor and realty listings to identify homes for sale. A real estate broker can add value to your search by providing information about the house and property, the neighborhood and its schools, recreational and cultural opportunities, and other costs and advantages of living in a particular area.

Increasingly, sellers are marketing their homes directly to save the cost of using a broker. A real estate broker typically takes a negotiable amount up to 6 percent of the purchase price, from which it pays a commission to the real estate agent. "For sale by owner" sites on the Internet can make the exchange of housing information easier and more convenient for both buyers and sellers. For example, Web sites such as Zillow.com serve home sellers and buyers directly. Keep in mind, however, that sellers acting as their own brokers and agents are not licensed or regulated and may not be knowledgeable about federal and state laws governing real estate transactions, potentially increasing your risk.

Once you have found a house, you will make an offer to the seller, who will then accept or reject your offer. If the offer is rejected, you may try to negotiate with the seller or you may decide to forgo this purchase. If your offer is accepted, you and the seller will sign a formal agreement called a purchase and sale agreement, specifying the terms of the sale. You will be required to pay a nonrefundable deposit, or earnest money, when the purchase and sale agreement is signed. That money will be held in escrow or in a restricted account and then applied toward the closing costs at settlement. The entire home buying process can be anywhere from 30 to 90 days.

Whether to buy a home or not ultimately depends on your personal financial picture and your overall financial goals. For example, let's say you are two or three years out of college. If reducing some credit card or student loan debit is a priority for you, then it would make sense to rent a smaller apartment and live with a roommate until you have achieved that goal. And, it is not uncommon for recent college graduates to live with their parents for several months or a year to increase savings before going out on their own.

Renting vs. Owning a Home

Like we discussed with buying a new or used car let's dig further into the rent vs buy decision for housing.

Advantages of renting include:

- Lower monthly payments. You are not paying property taxes and homeowners insurance.
- Mobility. If you are not settled in a job or have family commitments, renting provides you with the ability to move on short notice as most leases are for one year.
- Less responsibility. Renters of apartments usually have no responsibility for maintenance of lawns, clearing snow or exterior cleaning or painting. And almost no liability for injuries that occur on your property.

Disadvantages of renting include:

- Increasing costs over time. Rent usually increases over time with inflation whereas home mortgage payments are typically fixed for the life of the loan.
- Paying rent does not contribute to your wealth. As a homeowner you can increase your wealth as most real estate increases in value over time.
- No tax deduction for renting. The interest and property taxes paid on a mortgage are tax deductible and can reduce your annual tax payments.
- Restrictions on the use of the property. Apartment leases typically have restrictions on how many people can live with you, whether pets are allowed and how much noise you can make.

The housing market has made big news over the years with many people having to foreclose on their home because they could not afford to live there. Housing prices have had the most fluctuation over the last ten years than any decade in history. It should not be that way.

Here is my recommendation before you buy a home:

- Have all credit card or student loan debt paid off.
- Have enough savings to put at least a 20-25%% down payment on the purchase price of the home.
- Have a separate savings account called "home maintenance" before you move in and contribute monthly to this account as part of your budget and the true cost of home ownership.

Maintaining a home to your level of satisfaction takes money. Having money budgeted ahead of time will give you less headaches and frustration. You will have peace of mind and can truly enjoy living in your home as a result.

Insurance

Insurance should simply be viewed as your wealth protector and nothing else. Insurance can be purchased for your property and your home, your car, your health, and other major assets. In each case, you weigh the cost of the consequence of a risk that may or may not actually happen against the cost of insuring against it. Deciding what and how to insure is really a process of deciding what the costs of loss would be and how willing you are to pay to get rid of those risks.

For example, installing an alarm system in your home may reduce homeowners' insurance premiums because that reduces the risk of theft. Of course, installing an alarm system has a cost too. Risk management is the strategic trade-off of the costs of reducing, assuming, and shifting risks.

Property insurance is ownership insurance: it insures that the rights of ownership conferred upon you when you purchased your property will remain intact. Typically, property insurance covers loss of use from either damage or theft; loss of value, or the cost of replacement; and liability for any use of the property that causes damage to others or others' property.

For most people, insurable property risks are covered by insuring two kinds of property: car and home.

With the amount of money that you spend on your home and your car, it is important to make sure that these assets are protected. If you have financed the purchases of either of these, nearly all states require to carry insurance on them. This is the lender's guarantee of repayment should your home be destroyed by a fire or other disaster or your car getting wrecked during an accident.

Of course, it is not just your personal property that you need to insure. You also need to insure your health and even your own life! If you work for an employer, more than likely you are offered health insurance as a benefit through your employer. It is important to sign-up for this benefit since the cost is likely going to be reduced by using your company's health plan. Private insurance is possible and with the new Affordable Healthcare Act, all U.S. citizens are required to carry health insurance. If you are unemployed or self-employed or your company doesn't offer health insurance, you need to purchase private health insurance. The cost for private health insurance will depend on many factors, such as your age, location, overall health, and the coverage that you choose. Private insurance can be expensive, but it is important to have health insurance as the cost of not having insurance can be much higher if something happens to you.

Finally, these are major purchases and decisions that you need to consider carefully. Buying a home, purchasing a car, and having the right insurance protection for you and your assets are key areas to ensure your financial health in the future.

CHAPTER 8: ENTREPRENEUR MINDSET
A Must Have to Get Ahead With Money

Do you have dreams of starting your own business one day? Well, if you said, yes, you would not be alone. According to the Kaufman Foundation, over 51 percent of the millennial generation plan to start their own business versus work for an employer, and for those that are working for someone else, 71 percent of millennial employees have a dream of owning their own business. With today's technology, this generation is realizing that all you need is a computer and seed money to get started. This generation also seems to have a mindset that even if they fail, they will still have learned valuable lessons and the risk is worth it. The idea of Corporate America does not appeal to this generation; they have dreams of being the boss. Of course, part of having the confidence to start your own business comes from having control of your personal finances. In this chapter, we will explore the entrepreneur mindset and how this mindset, along with The Young Money Plan can help you realize your dream of being an entrepreneur.

Reasons for Increase in Entrepreneurs

So, what exactly is driving the millennial generation to not even consider a "regular" job and jump straight to becoming an entrepreneur? Well, there are actually several reasons for this transformational thinking. One of the top reasons is freedom, with 69% listing this as their number one reason. This generation looks for the freedom in being their own boss, making their own decisions, and determining their own fate. Over 66 percent of millennials noted that the ability to choose their own projects was a factor in wanting to be an entrepreneur.

This is a generation that thinks outside-the-box and would rather do things "their way" than being told another way is better. In a close third and fourth (63 percent and 62 percent, respectively), millennials also noted that having an unlimited income potential and control over their own work were two additional reasons for becoming an entrepreneur.[44]

In fact, according to data from the Millennial Branding and oDesk, nearly 60 percent of millennials surveyed consider themselves entrepreneurs already with ideas, capital, and plans laid out for ventures. Also, 38 percent of the surveyed said they would recommend working for a startup over completing a traditional degree. This mindset is certainly a different way of thinking than we have seen with the past generations. With past generations, the thinking was that a college degree was the gateway to financial freedom and stability.[45]

Not surprising, universities and colleges are not ignoring this trend. There is now more than 2,000 colleges across the U.S. that offer entrepreneurship programs. This is a major change from the mid-1980s when fewer than 500 entrepreneurship programs were offered in the U.S. Universities and colleges are catching up with the entrepreneur mindset of the millennials and are making necessary changes in order to convince these potential students to still attend school and earn a degree. In addition to the full entrepreneur programs, there are over 5,000 courses on entrepreneurship that are available throughout the U.S. with both online and traditional campuses offering the courses. This is a 20-time increase from 1985 when just over 250 entrepreneur classes were offered.[46]

The Role of Social Media and Technology

Change has certainly played a large role in the millennial entrepreneurial growth and there are no bigger factors than social media and advances in technology. From computers, tablets, and cell phones, the millennial generation grew-up with technology; basically since they were born. The Internet has played a major role in the increase of millennial entrepreneurs. Gone are the days of having to start a brick and mortar business. With technology, all they need is a computer and Internet access. Online businesses are less risky to start and online technology is an area that the millennial generation knows very well.

The rise of social media has also helped these entrepreneurs. Social media outlets, such as Facebook, Twitter, LinkedIn, and Pinterest offer these young entrepreneurs a new avenue for promoting their businesses and networking. Social media allows entrepreneurs to showcase their brands, find new prospects and make them customers, and grow a loyal community of supporters through their social media sites. And all of this is done with lower marketing costs and increased sales. This has created a win-win situation for the entrepreneurs. Of course, the millennial generation is not the only ones to embrace technology and social media in becoming entrepreneurs, but the millennials are the first generation that the U.S. has seen a major change in the thought-processes of possible careers.

The Reality of Entrepreneurship

The idea of being an entrepreneur does sound like the perfect situation. Of course, it is not all sunny skies for entrepreneurs. Owning your own business is a lot of work, has a great risk involved, and can lead to failure. As you read earlier, freedom is one of the reasons why millennials want to become a business owner. One should not forget that many times business owners, when first starting out, actually work harder and longer hours than they would at a "traditional job." The financial risk is also something to highly consider.

Entrepreneurs, starting out, do not have a monthly or bi-weekly paycheck to rely on; it is all about how hard they work to determine what they make in the months and early years. For some people, this is not a way to live, but for entrepreneurs, they accept the risks for the rewards that they feel is possible.

For some, the process can be very rewarding. The millennial generation has learned that initial failure does not mean failure forever. In fact, they see failure as a learning experience to try different routes to success the next time due to the next great idea. They have accepted the risks, and have gone after their entrepreneurial dreams. The journey of becoming an entrepreneur can teach you a lot about yourself. You will likely realize that you have more drive, knowledge, and passion about your business than anything you have ever tried before. There is something magical about creating your own business, working hard to make the idea into reality, and watching your business grow. You will learn how hard you can work, what you are made of, and you also learn who your true supporters in life and business truly are.

There are few stories of the "easy road" when it comes to being an entrepreneur, but the millennial generation and other entrepreneurs seem to agree that the "easy road" was never the road they were intended to take. I am sure you have heard the saying "You don't achieve your dreams by playing it safe." Taking risks won't necessarily benefit you in the near-term, but risk-taking will likely open up a world of opportunities that you have not even considered yet. This is the exciting part of taking the chance and becoming an entrepreneur; your dream idea today may not even be the business you own 10, 15, or 20 years from now!

When you are faced with the greatest risk that you ever may face, you learn how to handle pressure, deal with obstacles and learn to believe in yourself. Amazingly, unknown opportunities are often the result of risk-taking. Ask the most successful entrepreneur and he or she would likely say that the current success would never have been possible without taking risks. It is important to reframe risk as an opportunity versus always seeing risk taking as a path to potential failure. Taking the entrepreneurial risk also helps you stand-out and present yourself as a leader. We never know the path that we will end up on with our careers, so it is important to always present yourself as a leader and one that believes in your own ideas. If you don't, who will? Finally, and maybe most importantly, we learn from risk. Risk-taking provides an opportunity for discovering your abilities and experiencing more internal and personal growth than you ever thought possible.

The Economic Effect

We cannot discuss the reasons why more young people are becoming entrepreneurs without having a look at how the economy has changed the attitudes among young people. Many young people still in college or about to join the workforce have seen their parents lose their jobs during economic downturns, receive pay deductions, or have to take a job below their education and skill levels.

This has caused young people to take a step back and realize that they may not be able to rely on Corporate America for the financial stability they were hoping for. Many millennials now believe that the risk of starting their own business is less than the risk of working for a corporation. Many young people face stiff competition for jobs since more people are attending college and earning degrees than ever before. This means that having a degree, something that once set job seekers apart, is now considered a part of the "norm."

In addition, entrepreneurs have also led the way in the economic recovery. With the creation and ideas for new businesses, people are finding jobs, new businesses are created and the idea of entrepreneurship is booming. More people are also starting to think entrepreneurially in almost all facets of their lives; whether they are an employee or a business owner. It is important to learn to take risks, understand how money works (ie...Young Money Plan), and never stop growing and learning. These are traits that can help all of us succeed regardless of being a true entrepreneur. Many Americans and especially young people have learned that the days of having things handed to them are over. It is time to take a stake in our own futures to create the kind of life we want for us and our families going forward.

Industries and Opportunities Ripe For Success for Young Entrepreneurs

Because of the Internet and technology the game has changed for young entrepreneurs. Much less capital is required to start a business today. What has not changed and never will is the hard work required to be successful. No matter what business you elect to start a strong work ethic is required. If you have a viable product or service and can create real value for people or other businesses then your voice will be heard. The following are some growth industries for those who may want to strike it out on their own with low to moderate startup costs.

1. LANDSCAPE AND LAWN MOWING SERVICES. With an aging population these services will be required more and more. You will need $2,000 - $4,000 in equipment costs to start. If you have great customer service along with high quality results you can gain much referral business in short order. My second cousin and college roommate Marty Grunder of Grunder Landscaping in Dayton, Ohio started his business with a $25 lawnmower as a teenager. Several years later he started a separate leadership development company called Marty Grunder Inc! He helps other landscaping and green industry business owners and professionals maximize their revenue through sales, marketing and operations management training. Combined his companies generate revenues of a couple of million dollars per year.

2. FOOD TRUCKS AND STREET VENDORS. The food truck scene continues to strengthen and allows for entrepreneurs to create distinct food offerings to a growing market of food enthusiasts. In 2009, after just graduating from UCLA, Jennifer Green and Misa Chien started Nom Nom Food Truck. The two felt the greater Los Angeles area was lacking in authentic Vietnamese food. By generating a strong following on social media prior their launch, Nom Nom was successful in its very first year. Sales reportedly reached close to $1 million after year two. According to Forbes.com, initial startup costs for food kiosks on the street could be $5,000 while a high quality food truck business could run between $25,000 - $50,000.

3. HEALTH AND WELLNESS. Not only is health a major issue in this country the cost of healthcare continues to rise. Leading many people to eat healthier and corporations to offer more health related services to their employees to hopefully drive down their employee healthcare costs. Wellness coaching, disease prevention education, nutrition webinars, health fairs and motivational programs are just a few of the business offerings that small and big corporations alike are looking to provide their employees. Startup costs could range between $25,000 - $250,000 depending on the breadth of services your provide to individuals and businesses.

4. E-COMMERCE AND MOBILE. According to VentureBeat, a leading source for news and perspective on technology innovation, and Braintree, a leading processor of mobile and web payments there are many industries that are ripe for innovation. Mobile apps continue to grow which further increases the utility of our smartphone. We conduct search, communicate, shop, learn, navigate and much more on our phones today. There will always be needs to fill or create and e-commerce ideas will always be listened to.

Direct Sales and Network Marketing.

Growth continues to occur within direct sales and network marketing. Because of technology, the Internet and social networks it will only continue to climb. Direct sales are primarily defined as seller based whereby a product is sold to a customer and is usually a one-time sale (i.e. knives, jewelry, kitchen ware, water filters, etc.). The company you represent has a unique and high quality product (i.e. Cutco knives from Vector Marketing comes to mind since I have owned them for nearly 20 years).

Network Marketing refers to a business whereby one purchases a sample product kit or product sampler for little money (typically $100 - $500). You can sell product directly to friends, family, personal contacts, businesses and also recruit others to become distributors, consultants, associates, members, affiliates or independent business owners (IBO's). Additional sales bonuses/royalties can be earned on the sales of the people that you recruit creating a residual monthly income opportunity.

As with any success you find in life it will take hard work, passion and focus to be successful. I believe network marketing and direct sales as a whole will continue to climb because of game changing technology, ease of entry, low investment required and distinct product offerings that create real value for people. Young people today have a desire to find financial and personal success after witnessing some tough economic times among their parents. Young people also recognize Corporate America does not necessarily provide economic or job security.

I believe the key is finding companies that have longstanding, quality and ethical track records with exceptional product offerings in strong consumer product categories. Amway, NuSkin, Herbalife, Avon, Tupperware, Melaleuca and Pampered Chef come to mind. Some of these companies have been around for several decades. NuSkin, one of the youngest of the "old" has been around for over 30 years. While it took over 20 years for NuSkin to reach $1 billion in annual sales, in 2013 they surpassed $3 billion in sales. Because of international expansion and successful new product launches, NuSkin and some other well positioned direct sales and network marketing companies have seen similar strong growth over the last few years.

Direct sales and network marketing is not just about products. Two successful companies offering services to people include ACN and LegalShield. ACN is a 20 year old company that offers telecommunications and energy and other essential services to homes and businesses. From phone service, wireless, internet, television to home security, gas and electric, ACN independent business owners offer customers services they already have and are spending money on.

Over the last 40 years, LegalShield has offered individuals and businesses with affordable attorney access and other legal services at a fraction of what traditional legal services cost.

LegalShield offers advice and assistance on a variety of legal issues that most of us face at one point or another.

NuSkin, along with Avon, Herbalife, Usana, Tupperware, Mannatech, and a few others are publicly traded companies. Which means you can buy their stock if you feel their growth will continue for years to come and participate in their potential continued growth as an investor.

There is real opportunity for young people in direct sales and network marketing. To be successful you need to have a genuine passion for the product or service, a desire to help others succeed and a strong work ethic. I believe the future is bright for the industry as a whole.

Entrepreneurship and the Young Money Plan

One of the main objectives of The Young Money 5 Step Plan to Financial Success is to prepare you for the future. It is likely that you don't even know what you will be in the future, where you will be, or what you will need. That is even more reason to start preparing today for the unknowns, so when the day comes that you realize these areas in your life, you are prepared.

Following the Young Money Plan can create the enthusiasm, desire, and the confidence you need to start a business that you are passionate about. You may wonder why this is. Well, the reason is because you are now starting to think differently about money and how to manage it. You are going to take action to start saving money automatically by setting up multiple named saving accounts for normal life happens expenses and you are going to start investing money automatically per month!

Besides the fear of failure, one of the primary reasons why people do not go after their entrepreneurial dream is a lack of capital. There are a lot of people, who would love to give their business idea a try, but they simply have no money. Banks are even less likely to loan money to unknown businesses today, and other capital sources are not as common either. If you follow the Young Money Plan, you will likely have the money necessary because you invested your money 5+ years, developed strong interpersonal skills, and then had the seed capital necessary to start your dream job. And this was all possible because you managed your money and invested for this very moment that you always hoped would come.

When you decide to make good personal financial decisions now, this will benefit you should you become a business owner. Finance issues play a major role in the failure of many small businesses. The reason for this is many business owners simply don't know how to manage money. Consider this: if you don't know how to manage your own money, how would you manage a business' money? The answer is probably not very well. Learning the key concepts of money today will prepare you to make better financial decisions in the future.

From Chapter One, Step One is to make a decision to dream. Without dreams, what are you waking up for each day, working for, or striving for? The answer is probably nothing. That creates frustration. The decisions you make today will impact you for a lifetime to come. Taking control of your finances, saving money differently and investing automatically means taking control of all of your current and future dreams. The beauty of this is you don't even know how big your future dreams will actually be. And there is no greater feeling than knowing you will be prepared when the dream finally presents itself and you have the opportunity to make it reality. The Young Money Plan is more than just steps to enhance your financial future; the Plan is a chance to enhance your entire life.

CHAPTER 9
Young Money Plan in Action and 5 Point Checklist

I decided to shut down *Young Money* magazine in 2009 because young people were moving away from print media at a fast rate. In the fall of 2010, I decided to launch the Young Money LIVE! Financial Success Speaking Tour on college campuses. While I knew the magazine had been well received over the years by college students and those in their 20's on campus, I had no clue how a "personal finance event" on a college campus would turn out. I was quite anxious and nervous about our first tour. Would students engage with us at our event? Would they come hear me speak? Would they even care as they have many other concerns on their mind? I knew I would find out very quickly when we scheduled 25 campus events in the fall of 2010. Our first stop was at Eastern Kentucky University. Immediately after setting up our display on the grounds of their student union I knew we had something of value. Students, both men and women, traditional and non-traditional students came up to our display and told us of their money challenges and fears. "I need to know how to save money better" or "how do I begin investing" were popular comments and questions no matter what campus we were on.

We provided free giveaways along with our tour sponsors and they left our event with a new direction on how to manage their money. And they had fun in the process. The Young Money 5 Step Plan movement was on its way: one campus and one young person at a time.

Young Money LIVE! in Washington D.C. – Another Test

Our next stop in the fall of 2010 was at Georgetown University, George Washington University and Howard University. I honestly had some doubts about whether students at Georgetown and George Washington would be interested in our personal finance and money event. Tuition at both schools is well north of $50,000 for ONE YEAR! I had wrongfully assumed that most of these students came from wealthy families so I figured that learning how to manage and invest their money to create wealth and a purposeful life was not going to be a top priority for most of them. Who was I to teach and inspire this "elite" group about the Young Money Plan? Like the experience at Eastern Kentucky, I was pleasantly surprised. As with every campus stop students at Georgetown and George Washington quickly engaged with us throughout the day. After the presentation I gave at Georgetown I was struck with emotion as I walked off campus. I had tears coming down my face because my pre-judgments about these 18-22 year old "privileged" students was completely off base. They were tears of joy because I realized that the Young Money Plan can actually change lives. I was super pumped.

You could almost see the worry and anxiety about being financially successful and secure leave the minds of many in the room as I explained each of the five steps. Especially, when

I shared Step 5 on giving. It was as if there was a collective exhale in the room. The pressures that the world was putting on these students and all of us at times to be "successful" was starting to scatter into thin air. The students at Georgetown, George Washington and Howard University did not know about real goal setting and dreaming. Nor did they know how to create and track a personal budget, or how to automate saving and investing every month to create financial health and wealth. And also, how giving every month can add real joy and happiness to one's life and overall financial plan. It quickly became very apparent to me that the Young Money Plan can affect anyone no matter what economic or cultural background they had come from.

Young Money LIVE! in Chicago – The story of Michael

I have had the privilege to speak to thousands of millennials in 35 states since 2010. I have made several visits to Chicago area schools including DePaul University, University of Illinois Chicago, Triton College, College of DuPage, Dominican University, Chicago State University, Oakton Community College and Harold Washington College. Good schools and great people.

I have always enjoyed the events at Harold Washington College in particular. This two year city college is located in the heart of downtown and bustling Chicago.

Our third Young Money LIVE! event at HWC in 2013 was advertised to students and faculty this time around. One of the teacher's on staff, Charles McSweeney, came to hear me speak in the school's first floor auditorium. Afterward he asked if I could come back that same evening and share the Young Money Plan with his night class. I immediately said yes. The presentation to about 30 of his students, both young and old, went very well. After all of the students left his class Charles said to me, "Did you notice the young man in the blue shirt while you were speaking?" I said, "Absolutely, he was really locked in on what I was saying." Charles replied, "His name is Michael and he is a difficult student. He sometimes comes to class high on some kind of drug and it really frustrates me and makes me sad because he has a brilliant mind. He rarely sits still in class but he did not move an inch while you were speaking." I agreed with Charles and listened to this teacher's genuine interest in one of his students. You could tell he pours much into all his students. Charles thanked me for coming back to his night class to speak and then I headed off to the elevators to leave the school. Just as I got off the elevator on the first floor I saw Michael talking to a young woman in the atrium. I walked past him, smiled and exchanged glances.

As I walked out of the school on to a busy downtown Chicago sidewalk I heard this very loud and clear voice in my head say, "Go back in there and talk to Michael." As a Christian and believer in Jesus I am not one to say I hear God's voice often. I have always chalked up most voices as simply my own thoughts. This was completely different than my own thoughts this time around. The clarity was surreal yet pointed. After briefly hesitating I turned around and went back in the school. I went straight up to Michael and said, "I noticed how locked in you were when I was presenting in your class. I want you to know that you have every bit of what it takes to be very successful in your life. This 5 Step Plan can help you make a difference not only in your life but in the life of others." He was very wide eyed and so was the young woman he was talking to. Michael said, "Thank you, I really liked what you had to say." I replied "It was great to meet you", shook his hand and left the school for the second time in less than five minutes.

A few minutes later as I was almost to my car in a nearby parking garage I heard this faint, but getting louder sound of someone running. I quickly turned around and there was Michael running toward me. He stopped and, in shortness of breath, he said "Can I get your business card because I really want to change my life and learn even more about what you said". At the same time I gave Michael my card an elderly man walked up to me and asked if I had any spare change for a meal. I chuckled inside because I felt I was being tested with my own 5 Step Money Plan. I gave the man some money, wished him well and Michael and I shared a long smile together as a result.

Young Money LIVE! in Las Vegas

Beyond the glitz and lure of Las Vegas are two quality schools: UNLV and College of Southern Nevada (CSN). We have held Young Money LIVE! at both of these campuses twice a year for the last three years. Like Charles McSweeney from Harold Washington College in Chicago, there is another teacher who is going above and beyond for the sake of his students. Jeff Jones is an accounting and business teacher at CSN who accepted my invitation from a phone call in 2011 to bring our Young Money LIVE! event to his campus. As with nearly all two year community colleges the average age of students at CSN is higher than a traditional four year college or university. Jeff realized that life skills, such as personal finance was a big need and he was struck with the simplicity of the 5 Step Money Plan. Since 2011 we have reached well over a thousand students at CSN including a couple of hundred high school students who were bused in for our event. We now have great support from top school officials at CSN and UNLV and we continue to see many students who are locked on to the Young Money Plan with hope, excitement and purpose.

Young Money LIVE! in Miami

With over 125,000 students from across the world on eight campuses Miami Dade College is one of the largest colleges in the United States. I have had the privilege to speak to a very diverse student body at four of their locations including North, Homestead, Kendall and Wolfson campuses. In the spring of 2014 I spoke to nearly 150 students in a standing room only auditorium at their downtown Miami campus. There was tremendous energy in the room as students age 18 - 35 were gaining financial confidence and a new way to think about money. I estimated at least 25 different nationalities were represented within this very diverse and engaging group.

In the fall of 2014 we held the Young Money LIVE! event at MDC's North campus. The large lecture hall within the business school was filled near capacity. As a speaker you can tell fairly quickly who is zeroed in on your content and who has something else on their mind. One young man in his early twenties was responding with great enthusiasm from the moment Step 1 was introduced. I could see his own personal belief in himself start to rise especially when I talked about developing your WHY. His first name was Wookerson. I have seen the faces and heard the stories of many Wookerson's across the country. Faces of young men and women who settle on not being financially successful because they believe wealth and success are only available to a select few. The same faces who may let fear and self-pity control their mind and attitudes. And the same faces that put more emphasis on what the world can do for them instead of how they can make the world a better place by including giving as a part of their personal financial plan. Wookerson let me know how he felt after our event by going on to Twitter and tweeting "Young Money changed my life today." He thinks I made an impact on him. Well, he did the same for me.

I have traveled to big cities like Los Angeles, Dallas, Philadelphia, Phoenix, New York and Atlanta and to small towns like Truckee, Nevada, South Bend, Indiana, Tuscaloosa, Alabama and Greensboro North Carolina to present the Young Money 5 Step Plan. The location does not matter. Young people, as a whole, are thirsting to know what their purpose in life is and how to make sense of money.

Your 5 Point Checklist to Move Forward Now

Congratulations! You have made it to the end of this book. By doing so you have made it clear that you don't want the status quo with your financial future. So let's get rolling. Following is the 5 Step Plan action steps you can do next so you can begin your own personal Young Money Plan.

1. MAKE A DECISION TO DREAM. Start a dream notebook. Write down both your short term, mid term and long term dreams and goals.

Be specific. "I want to save a lot of money this year" or "I want to have a really nice car" is too general. Be specific with your dreams including the exact car you want to drive someday. It's also very important to make your goals personal and not necessarily what the world tells you is important or valuable. Money is personal and has different meanings for different people. Have fun going through this process. Dreaming and goal setting is the motivation to build financial confidence that can lead to a much fuller and richer life!

Examples of specific short term dreams and goals (1 -12 months out)
- I will save $75, $150, $300 or more within the next 30 days.
- I will have four named savings accounts set up in 90 days.
- I will save $2,000 in 6 months.
- I will save $4,000 in 12 months for down payment on a new or used car.

Examples of mid term goals (1 - 5 years out)
- I will save $5,000 within 18 months for a down payment on a new or used car
- I will pay off my new car loan of $10,000 in 16 months.
- I will save $4,000 in 18 months for my new apartment deposit and new furniture.
- I will save $2,500 in 3 years for a trip to Europe.
- I will save $25,000 in 5 years as a down payment for my first home.
- I will save $5,000 in 3 years to start my online business on the side

Examples of long term goals (10 - 25 years out)

* I will invest monthly for the next 10 years to accumulate $75,000 to pay off my first house.
* I will invest monthly for the next 8 years to accumulate $60,000 in order to start my dream business of a breakfast cafe. Or yoga studio. Or my new tech company, etc.
* I will invest monthly for the next 25 years to accumulate $1,000,000 to retire early or work part time only because I want to work not because I have to anymore.
* Post these goals and dreams where you can see it daily—on your mirror in your bathroom, your refrigerator or even both. Include these goals in the notes section of your smart phone.

2. SET UP YOUR AUTOMATIC SAVINGS PLAN. This is super easy and you will be so glad you did it.

* If you don't have a checking or savings account, open one up today by visiting a bank or credit union or opening online. Or through an online bank. There should be no cost to you to have either of these accounts.
* Have a predetermined dollar amount transferred from your checking to your savings account on a monthly basis AUTOMATICALLY. You can set it up on your bank or credit union website or tell them at the branch. You can choose any day of the month for the automatic transfer to occur like the 15th or 25th of each month. You can increase or decrease the dollar amount at any time.
* It does not matter the dollar amount you start with. By starting with only $10 you are creating a savings habit. That number will increase over time because you

realize how your savings account is helping you cover unexpected expenses that life brings to all of us.

- Eventually create multiple named savings accounts (or sub accounts) so you have the money on hand when life happens expenses happen to you such as traffic tickets, broken smart phone glass, car repairs, home repairs etc.. You can also set up separate named savings accounts for near short term needs and wants like: clothes/shoes savings account, entertainment savings account, future car savings account, travel savings account, future apartment savings account, emergency fund, giving etc. And remember to set up AUTOMATIC transfers from your checking to your savings accounts each month for these accounts.

3. CREATE YOUR PERSONAL SPENDING PLAN (BUDGET)

- Start today by tracking your spending and becoming AWARE of where your money is going. Record everything you spend for two weeks, then a month. It's as easy as snapping a cellphone photo of every receipt you get or jot down in your cell phone's notes area. This will give you a picture (literally) of where you are currently spending money.

- Identify the difference between your needs and wants. Before making any purchase, ask yourself whether it is a need or a want. Remember, needs are things you have to have to survive (food, water, housing, transportation, clothing) and wants are things you'd really like to have, but can survive without (video games, eating out instead of cooking at home, entertainment, second pair of running shoes, etc.).

* Know your average monthly income so you can compare your fixed and variable expenses. Making sure you have more income than expenses.

* Because you have identified your WHY and established some short term, mid term and long term goals it will become much easier for you to Say No Sometimes to things you think you NEED but ultimately just WANT.

4. SET UP YOUR AUTOMATIC INVESTMENT ACCOUNT

* I listed several companies in Chapter 4 that I recommend to use for your first investment account. Most of them have no minimum investment requirement.

* Get comfortable with some or all of them by visiting their website that I listed. Then if you want to get even more comfortable you can call their toll free telephone number listed on their website. They can give you guidance on which mutual fund or exchange traded fund (ETF) to begin with. I recommend growth mutual funds or the S&P 500 ETF to start.

* After you are comfortable and have completed Steps 1, 2 and 3 then open up an investment account.

* Elect to have an automatic investment plan established from the beginning by having $25, $50 or $100 or more AUTOMATICALLY transferred from your checking to your investment account every month. Just like Step 2 you can choose the 5th, 15th or 25th of each month.

- You have gone from a spectator to a participant in the game of investing. And you are taking advantage of "dollar cost averaging" by investing every month.

5. PAY YOURSELF SECOND BY GIVING FIRST

- Think about organizations, causes or charities that you would feel really good about giving money to on a regular basis. Perhaps it is a local fundraiser or project or your local church, or a local ministry or international ministry opportunity.

- A couple of organizations I like are PureCharity.com and JustGive.org. They provide a vast array of giving opportunities to support causes, non-profits and projects that are local to across the whole globe. And many may have a personal connection to you. Pure Charity also has an innovative way to increase your giving through Pure Charity rewards. By simply purchasing products that you use on a regular basis online through select national retailers a percentage of your purchase goes into a giving fund. Which you can use to give to other causes, projects, or non-profits.

- Once you have decided where to give set up AUTOMATIC giving just like you have done with automatic saving and investing. If giving is new to you start with as little as 2% or 5% of your monthly income. As you see the impact of your giving over time you may choose to increase your monthly giving percentage because of the impact and joy it is providing.

"MONEY PROVIDES TWO THINGS: COMFORT AND THE ABILITY TO GIVE MORE".

BOB PROCTOR

I also love how New York Times bestselling author John Maxwell puts it. "People say there are two great days in a person's life: the day they were born and the day you discover WHY".

My hope for you is that the Young Money 5 Step Plan to Financial Success will inspire you to seek out your true purpose here on earth and pursue it with much vigor and passion.

If this book has touched you or inspired you to think differently about money I'd love to hear from you. Please share your success, challenges and inspirations by emailing them to me at tromer@ youngmoneyuniversity.com. Hope we meet again and best wishes to your near and long term future!

ENDNOTES

1   *Twentysomething Inc. 2010 survey*

2   *Jessica Dickler, CNN staff writer*

3   *Charles Schwab's "Parents & Money" survey*

4   *Charles Schwab Survey*

5   *MediaPost Communications 2013*

6   *Forbes 2013*

7   *Money Matters On Campus Survey (2014) Administered By EverFi and Sponsored by Higher One*

8   http://www.housingwire.com/articles/26040-median-home-price-hits-8-year-high

9   http://www.thepeoplehistory.com/1942.html

10   http://www.investopedia.com/terms/c/compounding.asp

11   http://www.daveramsey.com/article/how-teens-can-become-millionaires/lifeandmoney_kidsandmoney/

12   http://www.daveramsey.com/article/how-teens-can-become-millionaires/lifeandmoney_kidsandmoney/

13   http://www.daveramsey.com/article/how-teens-can-become-millionaires/lifeandmoney_kidsandmoney/

14   http://www.investopedia.com/articles/07/stock-exchange-history.asp

15   http://www.investopedia.com/articles/07/stock-exchange-history.asp

16   http://www.investopedia.com/articles/07/stock-exchange-history.asp

17   http://www.investopedia.com/articles/07/stock-exchange-history.asp

18   http://www.investopedia.com/articles/07/stock-exchange-history.asp

19   http://www.investopedia.com/articles/07/stock-exchange-history.asp

20   http://www.investopedia.com/articles/07/stock-exchange-history.asp

21   http://www.investopedia.com/articles/07/stock-exchange-history.asp

22   http://www.investopedia.com/articles/07/stock-exchange-history.asp

23   http://www.investopedia.com/articles/07/stock-exchange-history.asp

24   http://www.investopedia.com/articles/07/stock-exchange-history.asp

25   http://www.investopedia.com/terms/s/stock.asp

26   http://www.investopedia.com/terms/s/stock.asp

27   http://www.investopedia.com/terms/s/stock.asp

28   http://www.investopedia.com/terms/m/mutualfund.asp

29   https://investor.vanguard.com/etf/?WT.srch=1

30   https://investor.vanguard.com/etf/?WT.srch=1

31   https://www.youtube.com/watch?v=YdcJSsRfL8s&list=PL8FE6A36103E4C6EB&index=

32   Proverbs 11:16, *New International Version*

33   Proverbs 22:16, *New International Version*

34   1 Tim 6:10, KJV

35   Ephesians 4:28, ESV

36   Sallie Mae 2009

37   Bureau of Labor Statistics 2011

38   Nelson, Lust, Story, & Ehlinger, 2008 http://www.ncbi.nlm.nih.gov/pubmed/18677880

39   Norvilitis et al. (2003)

40   *Charles Schwab*

41   *Charles Schwab Young Adults and Money Survey*

42   *Charles Schwab Young Adults and Money Survey*

43   *KeyBank and Harris Interactive*

44   http://www.entrepreneur.com/article/228464

45   http://www.entrepreneur.com/article/228464

46   http://www.entrepreneur.com/article/228464

65958650R00096

Made in the USA
Lexington, KY
30 July 2017